Even in Darkness

Even in Darkness

Judges and Ruth simply explained

Gordon J. Keddie

 EVANGELICAL PRESS

EVANGELICAL PRESS
Faverdale North, Darlington, DL3 0PH, England

e-mail: sales@evangelicalpress.org

Evangelical Press USA
P. O. Box 825, Webster, New York 14580, USA

e-mail: usa.sales@evangelicalpress.org

web: http://www.evangelicalpress.org

First published 1985
Second impression 1993
Third impression 2007

British Library Cataloguing in Publication Data available

ISBN 13   978-0-85234-201-5   ISBN 0 85234 201 2

Unless otherwise indicated, Scripture quotations are taken from the Holy
Bible, New International Version. Copyright © 1973, 1978, 1984 by
International Bible Society. Used by permission of Hodder & Stoughton,
a division of Hodder Headline Ltd. All rights reserved.

'NIV' is a registered trademark of International Bible Society. UK
trademark number 1448790.

Typeset by Inset, Chappel, Essex.
Printed and bound in Great Britain by Biddles Ltd, King's Lynn, Norfolk.

ACKNOWLEDGEMENTS

Heartfelt thanks are due to Dorothy McKissock and Dawn McKelvy, who typed the manuscript, and to the Rev. Dr Bruce C. Stewart, who made many helpful suggestions.

'Even in darkness light dawns for the upright, for the gracious and compassionate and righteous man' (Psalm 112:4).

'And what more shall I say? I do not have time to tell about Gideon, Barak, Samson, Jephthah, David, Samuel and the prophets, who through faith conquered kingdoms, administered justice, and gained what was promised; who shut the mouths of lions, quenched the fury of the flames and escaped the edge of the sword; whose weakness was turned to strength; and who became powerful in battle and routed foreign armies' (Hebrews 11:32—34).

'Do to them as you did to Midian, as you did to Sisera and Jabin at the river Kishon, who perished at Endor and became like refuse on the ground . . . May they ever be ashamed and dismayed; may they perish in disgrace. Let them know that you, whose name is the Lord — that you alone are the Most High over all the earth' (Psalm 83:9,10,17,18).

Contents

Index to Maps

Preface

Why has the book of Judges been so neglected in our day? Is it because we regard it as no more than a source of Sunday School Bible stories, suitable only for the simplest moral instruction of primary level children?

One thing is certain. Not many of us — including those with a lifelong connection with the church — have heard much about Judges since we grew out of Sunday School age. Even ministers who generally preach consecutively through Bible books tend to bypass Judges. Judges shares with Esther and the Song of Songs the dubious distinction of being thought less than worthy of the most careful attention by God's people. If, however, we believe that 'All Scripture is God-breathed and is useful for teaching, rebuking, correcting and training in righteousness' (2 Timothy 3:16), then we must realize that Judges has a vital place in the unfolding plan of salvation — as vital as any other in the mosaic of redemption history.

There may be a deeper reason for the neglect of Judges. It is a hard book about hard times. It deals with sin very explicitly, but, unlike pornography, which is the art of making sin attractive, it shows it in all its ugliness and repulsiveness. Furthermore, we are never left with the idea that we are somehow outside the story. These are not tales to tickle the ears. They speak to our consciences in our real life in the modern age. As Israel turned from God and needed deliverance, so we today need to be delivered from our backslidings. The message is all the more pointed, and therefore uncomfortable, because it speaks specifically to unbelief and hypocrisy within the covenant community, the church. While it is true that the heathen experience the wrath of a holy God in no uncertain terms throughout the period of

1

the judges, it is clear that the central thrust of the message is to the professing church of God. In New Testament terms, it is a challenge to those who profess to be Christians to live consistently with their profession of faith. In its own context, then, the book of Judges points to the need of God's people of that time for a living theocratic king who will lead them in faithful service to their God. This in turn paves the way for the raising up of that king in the person of David and ultimately in his antitype, the Lord Jesus Christ, the King of kings and Lord of lords.

The book of Judges speaks to all who are, by God's grace, given 'an ear to hear' God's message for our own day and our present condition, individually and as a nation. The message is one of the need for personal faith in the living God. And this, in the light of the whole Scripture, means nothing less than hearing Paul's words to the Philippian jailor: 'Believe on the Lord Jesus Christ and you will be saved.' The society in which we live gives abundant and appalling evidence of the kind of spiritual and moral decay which kindled the anger of God against his own people and the heathen nations around them. Three millennia have passed since then, but human nature is in the same need as ever it was. But the Lord has not changed either: Jesus has come and died upon the cross as the once-for-all sacrifice for sin. He has risen triumphant over death and the grave and reigns in glory as the Lord of all. His arm is not shortened that it cannot save. His message is one of hope and of victory for a darkening world.

Gordon J. Keddie
Wishaw,
March 1985

Outline

The book of Judges

I. Introduction (1:1–3:6)
    A. The incomplete conquest of Canaan (1:1–2:5).
    B. The condition of Israelite society (2:6–3:6).

II. The history of Israel under the judges (3:7–16:31).
    A. Othniel and the Syrian oppression (3:7–11).
    B. Ehud and the Moabite oppression (3:12–30).
    C. Shamgar and the victory over the Philistines (3:31).
    D. Deborah and the Canaanite oppression (4:1–5:31).
        1. The narrative of Israel's deliverance (4:1–24).
        2. The song of Deborah (5:1–31).
    E. Gideon and the Midianite oppression (6:1–8:35).
        1. Gideon's call and preparation (6:1–40).
        2. The victory over Midian (7:1–8:21).
            a. Preparation for battle (7:1–15).
            b. The battle at En-harod (7:16–22).
            c. Pursuit and final reckoning (7:23–8:21).
        3. Gideon's judgeship (8:22–35).
        4. Abimelech and the fall of Gideon's house (9:1–57).
            a. Abimelech's seizure of the throne (9:1–6).
            b. Jotham's curse (9:7–21).
            c. The fall of Abimelech (9:22–57).
    F. Tola and Jair save Israel (10:1–5).
    G. Jephthah and the Ammonite oppression (10:6–12:7).
    H. Ibzan, Elon and Abdon (12:8–15).
    I. Samson and the Philistine oppression (13:1–16:31).

3

The book of Ruth

Time-scale chart

The chronology of this period is not easy to determine with great certainty. Leon Wood (1975) has argued persuasively for a period of about 350 years, while others, like A. E. Cundall, beginning from a later date for the exodus and conquest, reduce this to under 200 years. The chart below follows the former opinion, but it must be borne in mind that by no means is this 'the law of the Medes and Persians, which cannot be altered'.

	BC	AD	
Samson	1050	1950	
1075–1055			Second World War
			First World War
Tola & Jair	1100	1900	
1119–1096			Queen Victoria
			(1837–1901)
	1150	1850	The Crimean War
Deborah			
1209–1169			Industrial Revolution
	1200	1800	
Ruth?			American Independence
			1776
Ehud	1250	1750	
1309–1229			The Great Awakening
	1300	1700	
			The Glorious Revolution
			1688
Othniel	1350	1650	Oliver Cromwell
1367–1327			
			King Charles I
Joshua	1400	1600	Authorized Version 1611
			King James VI & I
Moses			
Exodus c. 1446	1450	1550	Reformation in Britain

1.
Broken promises

Please read Judges 1:1–2:5; Joshua 23,24

'The angel of the Lord went up from Gilgal to Bokim and said, "I brought you up out of Egypt and led you into the land that I swore to give to your forefathers. I said, 'I will never break my covenant with you, and you shall not make a covenant with the people of this land, but you shall break down their altars.' Yet you have disobeyed me. Why have you done this? Now therefore I tell you that I will not drive them out before you; they will be thorns in your sides and their gods will be a snare to you"' (Judges 2:1–3).

The book of Judges strikes us at first glance as possibly the darkest book in the entire Bible. It records the significant events of some three and a half centuries of Israel's history, from the death of Joshua to the rise of Samuel and the establishment of the monarchy in Israel, i.e. from c. 1390 – c. 1050 B.C.[1] In so doing, it charts the decline of the covenant people of God as they increasingly depart from the commands and the blessings of God to give themselves over to the wickedness of the very peoples that they had been sent to destroy and supplant. From that perspective it is a sad story indeed. There is, however, a thread of blessing and of hope shining forth from this tapestry of national sin. It was a period in which God planned to govern his people by 'judges', whom he would sovereignly raise up and endow with spiritual power to be the instruments of revival. These were not judges in the modern sense, but were civil governors and often military leaders upon whom the

7

seal of God was placed. We are told that 'the Spirit of the
Lord' came upon some of them and it is evident that the
periods of relative peace and prosperity were often of con-
siderable duration. For example, Ehud's defeat of Moab
brought eighty years of peace to the land. Peace is not the
same as spiritual revival, but it seems clear enough that these
were times of a revived faithfulness of some kind. While
the book, then, certainly portrays human depravity in all
its viciousness — what can surpass Judges 19–21 in this
regard? — it also reveals the unfolding of the divine plan
of redemption and calls sinners to repentance. The message
of salvation to undeserving rebels is renewed, generation
after generation, underscoring the great mercy of the living
God and, sadly, the unyielding hardness of heart of the
generality of those who are supposed to be his own people.

In this fact there is a point that must not be missed if
we are to understand what the Lord is doing in this period.
Very often, in order to make application of this to our own
day, the expedient is adopted of substituting the name of
one's own nation for Israel. The idea is that what applies
to the nation of Israel carries over in our age to apply to,
let us say, Britain or the U.S.A. This is simplistic and mis-
leading, for a proper view of the unity of the Old and New
Testaments involves a proper view of the essential unity
of God's people in these two eras. Israel, then, is the church
of the Old Testament and the fact that it is a political entity
detracts from that not one whit. The application to our
own day is to the covenant people under the New Testament — to the church, those who by their own profession
and history have been in covenant with the Lord. We must
seek to see the lessons of Judges in terms of 'us' rather
than 'them' — of the church rather than modern nations.
The first call is to the Lord's people now upon earth to
be faithful to their covenant with God. It is also true, however, that there is a call to the unbelievers in every nation
under heaven. It is true that nations will perish under God's
judgement if they are given over to darkness and wickedness.
God, however, is not concerned with national boundaries
as much as he is concerned with the presence and power of

the church from place to place. There is 'one nation under God' and it is the holy nation, the royal priesthood, the elect church of God in Christ of every tongue and every race upon the earth. The fundamental application is to call that body to faithfulness against the awful background of the broken promises of God's people of old. They were, as one writer put it, 'all talk and no walk'. Will this also be the testimony of heaven against us? This is our challenge from Judges!

Sure promises

It was not for want of promises or evidences of divine power that Israel failed. According to promise they had been delivered from Egypt and brought to the promised land. By the end of Joshua's campaigning days much had been achieved and, although the coastlands and valleys still remained to be conquered, the Canaanites were terrified by Israel's victories and the 'momentum', as we might say, was very much with God's people (compare Joshua 11:16–23). When Joshua bade farewell to them, as recorded in Joshua 23:6–11, it was with the promise of God's power to finish the task. 'One of you routs a thousand,' he said, 'because the Lord your God fights for you, just as he promised. So be very careful to love the Lord your God' (vv. 10, 11). Subsequently, the covenant was renewed at Shechem, at which time Israel solemnly professed to be devoted to the will of God.

This latter episode is instructive in that, while it assumes the sure promises made earlier, it also reveals something of the cracks in Israel's faithfulness which were to widen into chasms later on. Joshua recounted the mighty acts of God in their behalf hitherto and, having done so, challenged them to choose whom they would serve (Joshua 24:15). Would it be the false gods they worshipped in Egypt, the false gods of the Canaanites or the Lord Jehovah? 'Why,' the people protested, 'the Lord, of course.' Joshua perceived that they protested too much and told them that they were

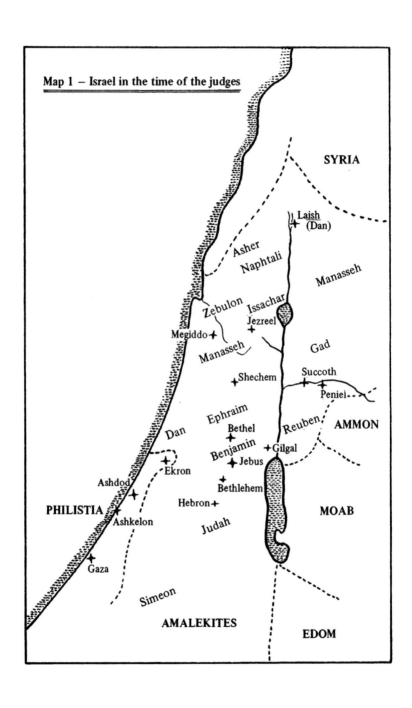

Map 1 – Israel in the time of the judges

unable to serve the Lord and that the Lord would make an end of them if they chased off after the Canaanite gods. In other words, he was telling them to make sure that they knew what they were doing when they so easily asserted their faithfulness (24:19). Still they affirmed their covenant (24:21) and so Joshua called for practical obedience in the casting away of their 'foreign gods' (24:23). Again they witnessed their engagement to be the Lord's servants (24:24) and so Joshua set up a stone to record their action. This would be a witness against them if they were untrue to the Lord (24:27) – an intimation of the fact, surely, that men are not so much condemned by what they simply do not want to do as by that which they so easily promise the Lord they will do, yet fail to deliver. How near we can draw to God with our lips while our heart is far from him! To all appearances, Israel was on the threshold of final triumph – but, alas, the triumph was not to be!

Selective obedience

Judges 1:1–2:5 is the first of two introductions to the chronicles of the judges. It recounts the negligence of Israel to carry out her commission and the subsequent rebuke administered by the Angel of the Lord. The second introduction, which extends from 2:6–3:6, covers much the same ground except that it does so more with an eye to the history of cyclical regression and revival to be unfolded in the body of the book.

We are told that Judah – with Simeon, whose territory was a number of cities in Judah's area – was first to go to war. They defeated Adoni-bezek (1:4–7). They seized Jerusalem (1:8), although it must have soon fallen back into Jebusite hands (Joshua 15:63). They gained many victories, for the Lord was with them (1:19), but 'they were unable to drive the people from the plains, because they had iron chariots' (1:20). The other tribes had more limited success still and, although they were able to put the subjugated Canaanites to forced labour, they apparently deliberately ignored God's command to destroy them.

It is clear enough that they were content, in the main, to restrict their conquests to the hills and also only to enslave rather than destroy the inhabitants. In the light of 2:1—6 and subsequent events, and remembering Joshua's anticipation of imminent apostasy, it seems inescapable to conclude that the Israelites did not want to destroy the Canaanites and their cities and did not wish to venture any campaign in the coastal plain where the added hazards of the 'iron chariots' would have to be faced. They were, in fact, directly disobedient to the Lord and their motive, as confirmed in Judges 2:12—23, was an openness to the false religions of the land. We are never militant in opposition to those sins which are secretly dear to us. Israel was compromised as the executor of the divine justice by simple unbelief in the living God and his precious promises!

Let us apply this to our own day. The church is commissioned to preach the gospel. This is her great task while the world lasts. With this is the promise of the blessing of God. To be sure, the church is not promised a set growth rate or level of success. It is not revealed to us who is to be saved or how many will be converted. There may be growth in the local church or there may be refining and testing. Yes, churches may even experience a *blessed* contraction! For all that that is true, however, the central theme of God's work is the outpouring of blessing upon his faithful covenant people. The church will cover the earth as the waters cover the sea and when we consider the invisible aspect of the church, namely the ingathering of the elect, then the church is indeed always being added to, since not one of these true believers can be plucked out of the hand of the Lord (John 6:37,38). History is seeing, with the translation of deceased believers to glory and the conversion of the lost in the church upon earth, the inexorable progress of God's work of redemption to the completion at Christ's return of the church of the first-born (Hebrews 12:22—24). The specific point of application is to ask: 'What are your expectations for the gospel? Is it an unfolding vista of victory? Or a gloomy holding operation? Is your church a stopping-off place for a few hardy folks who are in town for a while and want a cosy little fellowship? Or is your perspective that of conquest for Christ, of venturing for the lost in your community?

On the individual level a similar point may be made. Often professing Christians draw back in relation to personal holiness. There is almost a fear of being too holy. Actually it is a love for the old ways. Somehow the world would not be the same without some old-fashioned sin — or opportunities to sin — around. There is a tacit acceptance of organized sin in the world. Do you remember how Bishop Pike felt that prostitution, for instance, had some 'redeeming social value'? We don't want to disturb the alleged 'rights' of people to be wicked. We are rather in favour of the concept of 'victimless crime' — which is a completely anti-Christian notion, in point of fact. Sinners are at least victims of their own sins. The heart is so deceitful that Christians will not destroy the Canaanites of their own sins, because they have a recurrent desire to go back to them. Consider, then, the Lord's admonition to his professing people in Judges 2:1–5.

The chickens come home to roost

God's challenge and rebuke to Israel was brought by the 'Angel of the Lord', whom we believe to be the second person of the Trinity.[2] He came from Gilgal to Bokim (2:1). It is put this way, not to indicate his itinerary, but to remind Israel of the last time that he had come to his people, namely, just after the renewal of the covenant sign of circumcision at Gilgal and prior to the taking of Jericho (Joshua 5:13). The same Angel of the Lord who gave them their former conquests now came to deal with their covenant-breaking.

Israel had disobeyed God. They had neither destroyed the Canaanites nor kept themselves from false gods. The Lord told them that he would not drive out the Canaanites and that they and their false gods would be a trouble and a snare to them (2:3). They were without excuse. Their

sin now became their punishment and in this are two points
of universal applicability. First of all, if we will not do the
work of God when he has commanded us to do it, then he
will not do it for us. The devil will not flee from us, if we
decline to obey the Lord's injunction to resist him (James
4:7). We will, in other words, inevitably fall into our own
sins — they shall, as the Bible says, 'find us out' (Numbers
32:23). In the second place, there is very frequently a
residual and abiding effect of sin, in spite of the fact that we
may have repented of it and have been cleansed of it as to
its guilt and penalty as regards salvation. Israel had a 'thorn
in the flesh' to remind her of her disobedience. Sin leaves
its marks and only death and resurrection will eradicate
them. Our corruptible, our dying flesh reminds us of our
sins, and our particular weaknesses, even when triumphed
over in Christ, remain somehow attached to us and recall
to us our utter dependence day-by-day upon the Lord for
salvation from our sins. That is why the true Christian
always is longing for heaven, for there is the work of
redemption to be completed in us, and only there, with
Christ, our Saviour.

The response of God's people (2:5) is as instructive as
it is heart-rending. First there was sorrow for sin, touchingly
signalized in the name given to the place of confrontation —
Bokim, literally 'weepers'. Men weep for many reasons —
laughter, separation, bereavement, anger — but least of all
for their sins. When did you last weep as you considered
your sins? When were you last 'stricken' while in prayer?
This is the beginning of a real devotion and of blessed com-
munion with the Lord . . . a sense of helplessness, of need
and of a lack of any deserving of blessing by reason of having
offended a holy God. The second element is that of appealing
to the mercy of God. Israel 'offered sacrifices to the Lord'.
Here the Christological heart of the whole book of Judges
comes into focus. Israel fled to the Lord for grace and
forgiveness and in the presence of the eternal Son of God,
the 'Angel of the Lord'. This same eternal Son, only made
flesh in the person of Jesus Christ, is our Saviour. Now in
the risen Christ is redemption revealed in its fulfilled glory.

The shadow of Bokim is now the substance at Calvary. 'Weeping may remain for a night, but rejoicing comes in the morning' (Psalm 30:5). When the chickens (of our sins) come home to roost (in the rebuke of our Lord) we should give thanks, because mercy is offered and a Saviour is revealed to us. Have you little but a catalogue of 'broken promises' to show before the Lord? Then return and repent. Flee to Christ. He is the sacrifice for sin and he will not despise the broken spirit and the contrite heart (Psalm 51:17). This was the Lord's message to Israel and it is his message to us all.

Questions for further study:
1. Why was a successor to Joshua not appointed? (1:1,2.) How was Israel to discover the Lord's will? (Compare Judges 20:18—28.)
2. What do you make of the way Adoni-bezek was treated? (1:4—8.) Why were the Canaanites to be annihilated?
3. Review the performance of the various tribes. What was right and what was wrong in their actions in the campaign? (1:9—36.)
4. Compare the events at Gilgal (Joshua 5:1—15) and Bokim (Judges 2:1—6) respectively. Who was the Angel of the Lord? What is the ultimate significance of the latter passage for us?
5. Consider the application of the passage to God's people in every age:
    a. broken promises/covenant breaking — its nature and effects;
    b. the 'thorn in the flesh' — its meaning and purpose;
    c. rebuke and conviction of sin — their place in our lives;
    d. sacrifice for sin — who is our sacrifice and what is our duty under the gospel of Christ?
6. How is the church to approach the world? What are our expectations to be? What are the promises of God? What are our responsibilities?

References
1. For a thorough discussion of the chronology, see L. Wood, *Distressing Days of the Judges,* Grand Rapids: Zondervan Publishing House, 1975, pp. 10—17.
2. See chapter 7, pp. 56—62.

2.
False gods

Please read Judges 2:6–3:6; 17:1–18:31

'Then the Israelites did evil in the eyes of the Lord and served the Baals. They forsook the Lord, the God of their fathers, who had brought them out of Egypt. They followed and worshipped various gods of the peoples around them. They provoked the Lord to anger because they forsook him and served Baal and the Ashtoreths' (Judges 2:11–13).

The first of the two introductions to the book of Judges (1:1–2:5) records in some detail the failure of Israel, after the death of Joshua, to occupy all the land that God had promised to them. This was attributed not to a lack of numbers or military hardware — both factors heavily in the Canaanites' favour — but to simple disobedience to God's will. Israel broke her promises to obey the Lord and, therefore, as a covenant-breaker, forfeited the blessings promised in that covenant. This is the first and fundamental indication of the pattern of national backsliding which characterizes Israel's first three centuries in the land of promise.

The second introduction (2:6–3:6) covers much of the same ground, but anticipates the account of the various judges who figure in 3:7–16:31. It also touches upon the two principal areas of sin in Israel. The first is false worship, culminating in the worship of Baal (2:10–15), while the second, to be dealt with in our next chapter, is the disruption of order in society (2:16–19). These arose in the period between the passing of the elders who were with Joshua and the rise of Othniel, the first judge. To illustrate

17

these developments two case histories are included in the
'appendix' to the book (Judges 17–21). Both are clearly
from this early period[1] and are designed to impress upon
us the rapidity with which Israel declined as a people
supposedly devoted to God. The first of these is found
in Judges 17 and 18 and is illustrative of the drift away
from the true worship of the living God, which, in the
long run, always tends to culminate in an entirely false
religion. We need, therefore, to examine this story most
carefully.

Creative worship

The first part of our story, recorded in Judges 17, concerns
an enterprising fellow from Ephraim named Micah. He had
apparently stolen a large sum of money from his mother,
namely 1100 shekels of silver (i.e. 450 ounces). This must
have been an immense sum of money for those days. The
mother had roundly cursed the unknown thief, presumably
invoking the judgement of God upon him, and Micah,
evidently worried about this, restored the money to her.
She then consecrated it to the Lord for Micah to make
idols (17:3) and gave him some 200 shekels (eighty ounces)
which were fashioned into 'the image and the idol' – one
carved, the other cast (17:4). Micah had a private shrine,
literally 'a house of gods'. There he kept his idols and there
he had one of his sons serve as a priest. It must have bothered
him that he did not have a Levite for his priest, because
when a Levite did appear one day, looking for a place to
settle, Micah offered him the job of family priest at ten
shekels *per annum* plus room, board and clothes. The Levite
found this to be an offer he could not refuse and so he
accepted. Micah installed him and was evidently very pleased
with the arrangement, for he said to himself, 'Now I know
that the Lord will be good to me, since this Levite has
become my priest.' After all, he no doubt reasoned, he had
his own place of worship, his own gods and now his own
full-time Levite chaplain. Had he not proved his devotion
to the Lord far beyond the ordinary?

It is at this point that the tribe of Dan comes into the picture. In Judges 18 we learn that the tribe was looking for a territory of their own (18:1). Dan had been allotted the coastal plain, where modern Tel Aviv is situated, but they had failed to oust the Amorites (1:34) and were now 'squatters' on Ephraim's territory. A scouting party was sent to look for a suitable place. On the way they stopped at Micah's place and consulted his Levite, who told them what they no doubt wanted to hear, namely, 'Go in peace, your journey has the Lord's approval' (18:6). Subsequently they found the city of Laish in the rich Huleh valley near the slopes of Mt Hermon. They returned with the recommendation that Laish be seized and soon that part of the tribe that wanted to go through with the project set out on its expedition. They also stopped at Micah's 'house of gods'. This time, however, it was not to consult the Levite but to steal him, and Micah's idols, and use them to establish their own centre of worship in Laish. Micah was left, of course, with an empty chapel. The Danites then went on to destroy Laish and rebuild it as the city of Dan. Their new centre of worship was set up – essentially in opposition to the proper worship of God at Shiloh – and was led by priests of the line of Moses, starting with his grandson Jonathan. This rival worship continued up to the time of Samuel and was repeatedly revived during the period of the northern kingdom of Israel.

What are we to glean from this complex of events? Let us suggest at least three areas of significance.

First of all, there is evidence of a disturbing moral laxity among the people. They thought but little of the sinfulness of stealing. This is true of Micah, his mother and the Danites. Micah stole a small fortune and only returned it out of fear. His mother did not even rebuke him – in fact, she almost rewarded him. Later the Danites brazenly robbed the hapless Micah and, though we might consider it a just reward for his rotten behaviour, it was still a sin and one of which the Danites were quite unashamed (18:23). The application to our own day is obvious. It is also significant that it was done in the name of devotion to the Lord! (17:2,3; 18:19.)

Secondly, there is evidence of an increasingly open disobedience to the revealed will of God. The movement of the
Danites is a prime example. God told them to destroy the
Amorites (2:23). They failed because of a lack of trust
in the Lord. Then they compounded their faithlessness by
seizing an area not given to them by the Lord. This is always
the way of sin, is it not? We cover the effects of one sin by
committing another; we add lie to lie and build a mountain
of provocations before God!

Thirdly, we see the evil fruit of innovations in worship.
Micah and the Danites and the Levite who served them
both were in breach of God's law on four points. That is
to say, whereas God had appointed clearly how he was to
be worshipped, they felt free to modify his pattern for
worship.

1. They made and used images, whereas God had
   strictly prohibited such practices (Exodus 20:4).
   Micah intended that these idols only be aids to
   the worship of Jehovah. This was, however, only
   to open the door to worshipping the idols themselves. Hence the comprehensive scope of the
   second commandment.

2. They established private centres of worship, whereas
   God had commanded one place for all the people
   and that was then at Shiloh (Deuteronomy 12:1–7;
   16:1–7). There the ark of the covenant was located
   in the tabernacle from the wilderness. Ah, but how
   much more convenient to stay at home, with
   no long and wearying journey and no troublesome
   and independent-minded priest to prick our
   consciences! God wanted his family in the 'church'—
   at Shiloh. Micah and the Danites wanted the
   'church' in the family!

3. They appointed priests improperly. Micah appointed
   his son and then the Levite. The Danites, in their
   turn, employed the Levite and then priests of the

line of Jonathan, son of Gershom, Moses' son. These all contradicted the express will of the Lord (cf. Numbers 8:5–26; 18:1–7).

4. Related to this is the very movement of the Levite (Judges 17:8). He knew that God had appointed one place for him to serve and certain Levitical cities in which he could dwell (Numbers 35:1–8; Joshua 21:20–40). This false minister knew better than the Lord. God had given him a job and a place of work but he would look for work on his own! He was a 'career man' intent on making as good a living as possible. So he went his own way in spite of God's revealed will!

Such then was the 'creative worship' of Israel in those days. No doubt many, like Micah, believed that God was leading them to new forms of worship; to new, improved, expressions of praise; to bigger and more spectacular ways of presenting the gospel. Does this not cause us to ask ourselves the question, 'Are we, in the way we worship God, doing what God wants us to do?' This involves us immediately in some hard questions. For example, he has given us his divinely inspired 'Book of Praises' – the literal title of the Psalms. Yet, the Bible's own songs of praise have been left out of the praise of so many Christians. At the same time, we see a constant push for novelty, sometimes with all the razzmataz of show business: Christian 'rock', Christian acrobats, clowns parachuting into church services, professional choirs singing oratorios – the list is endless. Should we not ask ourselves the question: 'What has God *said* about the way we are to worship him?' Is God's Word silent on this point? Surely not! He certainly prescribed exactly the worship of Israel and the principle thus established comes to its free and full flowering in the worship of the New Testament church (John 4:23; Matthew 26:30; Acts 16:25; Ephesians 15:19; Colossians 3:16; James 5:13). Is God's Word not good enough after all? Are the promised blessings for *obedience* not sufficient for modern Christians?

The evils of false religions

The inevitable result of adding to and/or subtracting from God's revealed will is to fall prey to a false gospel. 'New light' is just 'old darkness' in a modern alluring garb. Israel, attracted by the outward aspects of Canaanite religion, which included both the 'convenience' of personal household gods and a loose attitude to morals, began by borrowing a few of the trappings but soon graduated to a full-fledged embracing of the false gods themselves. The Baals were the gods of the earth and of the weather – the guarantors of good crops. These were the first to be adopted. Then came the Ashtoroth, the male and female deities, whose worship involved ritual prostitution. Ashtoreth, the singular of the plural Ashtoroth, was probably the Assyrian goddess Astarte, or Ishtar, from which our word 'Easter' is derived.

A number of significant lessons are to be derived from this awful descent into open wickedness – lessons which are only too relevant in our own increasingly permissive age.

First is the fact that when people turn away from the Lord, they do not usually become atheists or libertines. In fact, they generally cling to the traditional institutions of religion and to the language of orthodoxy, while seeking in the meantime to effect the doctrinal and practical adjustments that will grant them maximum latitude with minimum loss of status and security. So it was in the day of the judges and so it is today!

Second is the amazing confidence of God-denying people in the very face of eternity. One might have thought in the circumstances that the Israelites would have more fear of the wrath of God against their clear rebellion. Yet their confidence – false as it is – is boundless. Micah is a classic case of a man being fully satisfied, fully at peace and fully expectant of God's blessing, while all the time being spiritually dead and under the condemnation of the Lord.

Third is the picture we are given of the terrible fragility of human society. If the Lord is not pleased to revive his cause and kingdom in any community, the potential for

that community sinking speedily into a degenerate condition
is staggering. Israel of old is not any nation, of course; it
is the church of God. Who will deny that the professing
churches of our day have been in precipitous spiritual
decline? With the increasing sanction given in the 'main-
line' churches to the grossest of sins, we are seeing the
'church' transformed into 'Sodom'. The 'house of the Lord'
has become the 'synagogue of Satan' (Revelation 2:9).
And what will happen in a society where the professed
followers of God are in fact doing the work of the devil?
This is what the book of Judges is designed to answer.

The revival of the church

Christ came not to call the righteous, but sinners. Paul
tells us that where sin abounds, there does grace much
more abound. We must seek the reviving power of Christ
in the church and in this way the gospel will certainly trans-
form the world. Do we need revival less than Israel of old?
Do we need the Holy Spirit in lesser measure? Are we so
abounding in the love of Christ and in the gifts of the Spirit
that we need not become excited about the reformation
of the church?

Perhaps we are discouraged by all this talk of spiritual
decline and the portents of God's just wrath. Well, the
promises of God are still sure and certain. The purpose
of the gospel still stands. The victory of Christ is accomplished. So let us embrace the 'good news' of Christ with
fresh resolve! Let us call on God that out of his great love
he might turn back those who tread the 'broad way that
leads to destruction' and bring them to the risen Christ,
who gave his life for sinners, that they become the children
of God and fellow-heirs with him.

Questions for further study:
1. Why did a generation grow up who 'knew neither the
   Lord nor what he had done for Israel'? (Judges 2:10.)

What fundamental responsibility had been neglected in Israel?

2. Review the story of Micah and the Danites and get a clear grasp of the facts.

3. Consider Micah's theft of his mother's money and her response. What happens to the concept of *sin* in a society where the teaching of God's Word is neglected or ignored? How should we respond?

4. Consider the movement of the Danites (and the Levite) in relation to God's revealed will. What characteristic of sin does this illustrate?

5. What are 'innovations in worship'? Why do we think Micah was wrong in believing God approved of his arrangements? What do we mean when we say that our worship should be controlled by the teaching of the Word of God? (Leviticus 10:1,2; Deuteronomy 12:32; Psalm 95:1; John 4:22–24; Acts 17:2; Romans 1:21–25.)

6. List the four particulars in which Micah and the Danites modified God's plan for worship. Consider the implications of this for our worship today. Do we need to change anything? How should we change, to give the glory to God?

7. What were the Baals and the Ashtoroth? Why do subtle shifts from the teaching of God's Word inevitably lead to false religion? Consider Paul's statement about 'a different gospel' in Galatians 1:6–10.

8. Consider the problem facing the churches in our day and God's answer to these problems.

Reference

1. In Judges 20:28 we are told that the high priest was Phinehas, the son of Eleazar, the son of Aaron. Phinehas therefore was active *before* the conquest (Numbers 25:7,11).

3.
A collapsing society

Please read Judges 2:16−23; 19:1−21:25

> *'Then the Lord raised up judges, who saved them out of the hands of these raiders. Yet they would not listen to their judges but prostituted themselves to other gods and worshipped them. Unlike their fathers, they quickly turned from the way in which their fathers had walked, the way of obedience to the Lord's commands'*
>
> (Judges 2:16,17).

If the first and primary sin of Israel was its turning from God to serve 'dumb idols', then the second great area of decline was the catastrophic slide into moral and civil anarchy. There was a breakdown of law and order such that wickedness was no longer restrained or punished. Israelite society was in a state of moral collapse. The case history which illustrates this is recorded in Judges 19−21 and the Lord's assessment of the situation and his solution to the problem is outlined in Judges 2:16−3:6. The situation was a grave one, as we shall see, but let us not forget that the message of the book of Judges is one of grace in the midst of sin and not merely a catalogue of the excesses of wicked people. There is a message of grace, of salvation and of revival for God's people, and we do not begin to understand the period of the judges until we grasp this fact. Ultimately we are, you see, pointed to Christ, the true Deliverer of the Israel of God − that is to say, the only Saviour of sinners.

The breakdown of the rule of law

The last three chapters of Judges are definitely not for
the faint-hearted. They record a story of moral depravity
unequalled in all of Scripture. From beginning to end they
form a catalogue of breaches of God's law. Israel's backsliding had accelerated until immorality was epidemic. This
was to culminate in mass murder and the breakdown of the
rule of law. The passage falls naturally into three sections.

First we are told the grisly story of the rape-murder of a
Levite's concubine (19:1–30). There was a Levite from the
same area as Micah (Judges 17:1; 19:1) and he had a concubine — in modern terms, he lived with his girlfriend. She,
however, had left him and 'gone home to daddy' in
Bethlehem. The Levite wanted her to come back, so he paid
her a visit to persuade her to return, which she did. It was
late in the afternoon before they set off north for Ephraim
(19:9,10) and they had to stop at Gibeah, a town of
Benjamin. They found no hospitality from the Benjamites,
however, and it fell to an old man from Ephraim, finding
them in the town square, to take them in for the night
(19:12–21).

It was at this point that the Benjamites started to express
an interest in the Levite. A group of evidently homosexual
Benjamites beat upon the old man's door declaring a desire
for sexual relations with his visitor (19:22). The old man
told them that they should not be so vile towards his guest
and he offered his own daughter and the Levite's concubine
to them for the satisfaction of their lust! He evidently felt
that their rape of his own daughter was preferable to their
sodomy with the Levite! As it happens, the men wanted
the Levite, so they refused the old man's suggestion. The
Levite, however, was apparently quite determined that they
would not get him, so he cast his concubine upon their
not-so-tender mercies, whether or not they wanted her.
She did indeed turn out to be acceptable to them for they
'raped her and abused her throughout the night' (19:25).
Next morning, the Levite found her dead on the doorstep.
He took her body home, divided her into twelve pieces

and sent one to each of the tribes of Israel in a call for retribution for this dreadful atrocity (19:26–30).

Secondly, we are told about Israel's reaction — the genocide of the tribe of Benjamin (20:1–48). There was strong and immediate action. 400,000 men assembled at Mizpah and a call was issued to the Benjamites to hand over the guilty men. Benjamin refused — no doubt out of a perverted sense of loyalty — and civil war was the result. Two battles took place, with Israel suffering defeat at the hands of Benjamin's relatively small army (26,700) and losing 10% casualties in the process (40,000). The third time, having the promise of victory from the Lord, Israel succeeded in taking Gibeah and putting Benjamin to flight. The vengeance of Israel was as thorough as it was unconscionable. All but 600 of the men of Benjamin and all of the women and children were put to death.

We should notice that Israel did seek the Lord's will in this sad business (20:18,23,27,28,35). He did give them specific answers to their questions. This guidance was not so much the Lord's *approval* of the project as his means of using it to chasten and humble both sides in the conflict. Both sides had over-reacted to the original incident — overreacted in pride. This the Lord purposefully corrected and the sheer scope of that correction testifies to the enormity of the spiritual darkness in the hearts of the people.

The third section deals with the reconstruction of the tribe of Benjamin (21:1–25). Israel had a serious problem. She had all but reduced the nation to eleven tribes. Benjamin had 600 men and no women and Israel had rashly sworn at Mizpah not to allow any of her daughters to marry into Benjamin (21:1). Benjamin seemed doomed to extinction.

Israel had taken another rash and immoral oath, however, and this they now exploited for the sake of Benjamin. They had sworn to kill any Israelites who did not muster for the war with Benjamin (21:5). No one had come from Jabeshgilead, east of the Jordan. An expeditionary force was swiftly dispatched with orders to fulfil the terms of this (sinful) oath . . . almost. They were to take care not to kill the virgins of that town so that they could be given as wives

to Benjamin. This provided only 400 wives and so Israel
then sought a method of providing for 200 more. This
latter instalment was made up in an equally unsavoury way.
Israel connived with Benjamin by turning a blind eye to the
kidnapping of 200 girls from the 'annual festival at Shiloh'
where the tabernacle was located. Israel reasoned thus:
since Benjamin *took* the 200 girls and Israel *did not give*
them to Benjamin, the first Mizpah oath was not violated!
This is, of course, a classic example of explaining away a
problem. Well did the writer of the Judges say, 'In those
days Israel had no king; everyone did as he saw fit' (21:25).

Right in their own eyes

The pervading impression is surely one of utter spiritual
and moral blindness. They did what was right in their own
eyes rather than that which is (truly) right . . . in the eyes
of God. What, then, can we glean from this wretched series
of events? Notice four areas of significance — the marks of
a collapsing society.

There is, in the first place, *widespread sexual immorality*
and this is signalized by the prevalence of open homosexuality. The terrible fate of the Levite's concubine puts
this in perspective. These men were of the vilest sort. They
had no shame. Their lusts were totally unrestrained. Consequently their preference for the Levite guaranteed the
terrible treatment of the Levite's concubine. To fail to
satisfy desire by the proper means leads inevitably to the
more brutal attempt to satisfy that lust by improper means
(cf. Exodus 20:14; Leviticus 18:22; Romans 1:26,27). The
basic problem of homosexuality is that it is a rejection and
reversal of God's definition of, and purpose for, human
sexuality. In common with all perversion of God's plan for
human relationships and personal moral behaviour — and we
include heterosexual sin in its various forms as well — this is an
offence to a holy God who made us to be his image-bearers
in the world. God's Word makes it clear that unashamed
sexual sin — open licentiousness in the streets and among

the civil and religious leaders — is the harbinger of the outpouring of God's wrath. Remember Sodom and Gomorrah,
as well as Gibeah of Benjamin, and remember also the words
of our Lord when he said of those who utterly reject the
gospel of his grace: 'I tell you the truth, it will be more
bearable for Sodom and Gomorrah on the day of judgement than for that town' (Matthew 10:15). The Lord places
a choice before men: will it be retribution or will it be
redemption?

A second mark of a collapsing society is *a corrupt ministry
in the churches.* The Levite was living in sin. He ought not
to have entered an adulterous relationship. It is apparent,
however, that sexual sin had become common and even
socially acceptable in the ministers of God!

The degeneracy of the ministry is seen too in the apparent
silence of the then high priest, Phinehas, on the issues of the
day. Phinehas (20:27) was a grandson of Aaron. His birth
is recorded in Exodus 6:25. In the past he had been a warrior
for the Lord's cause. In Numbers 25:7 we are told that he
took a spear in his hand to execute God's revealed judgement against Israel's immorality with the Moabite women!
According to Numbers 31:6, Phinehas led Israel against
the Midianites! He had seen the mighty acts of God and had
served the Lord with fearlessness and power, but where
was this mouthpiece of the Lord when Israel was mass-
murdering her own people? The ministry of God was weak,
unbelieving, compromised by its own sin, defeated, without
a message of salvation and without an eschatology of
victory . . . in other words, devoid of a living faith in the
Lord.

Surely this must drive us to prayer for the revival of
the church in our own day? I mean the 'church' in the
broadest sense. I mean the largely liberal churches which have
declined so disastrously in recent decades. I mean also all
those bodies of Christians who have adhered to a sound
biblical creed and have preached the true gospel of Christ.
Surely our prayer must be that every pulpit might herald
the unvarnished truth of God's Word and that the people
might believe in the Lord Jesus Christ and live sacrificially,

fearlessly and righteously in him! On a personal level, let it be asked, 'Do you pray for the revival of your church? Do you pray for the faithfulness of your minister? Do you pray for gifted men to be raised up for the ministry? Are you pleading with God that his messengers will be kept uncompromised and fearless in their ministries? Are you ready to see the issues of the day addressed from the Bible? Are you prepared for reproach, for mockery and for suffering for Christ's sake? Will you pray for the reviving hand of God?'

A third mark of a collapsing society is *a low regard for human life.* From the Levite's pushing his concubine into the hands of the men of Gibeah to the carnage of the civil war that followed, we have incontrovertible evidence of a low attitude to loss of life. In fact there was a love of killing. Killing was in effect translated into a virtue. Benjamin must die; Jabesh-gilead must die — a solemn oath demanded it!

We live today in a time of mounting viciousness. From abortion as a method of 'birth control' (a euphemism, incidentally, for birth prevention!), through terrorist bombings in market-places and hotels to the genocide of Uganda and Cambodia, a tide of callous indifference to the taking of human life is sweeping over our world. It touches us all and we must not imagine that we are unaffected. The more we are bombarded with violence, misery and death in news-papers and on television, the less we are horrified by that misery. Perhaps we look at it and shrug in resignation. Perhaps we turn off the TV and prefer not to think about it. Surely we must bear a testimony to the Lord's will in these matters and labour for the revival of godliness in our time. Only in Christ is life known for what it really is — God made us in his image to bring pleasure to himself. Christ is that perfect image. He is the pattern. In him is realized the meaning of life and in him it is to be enjoyed in all its fulness.

A fourth mark of a collapsing society is *the abdication by civil government of its duty to uphold the principles of God's law.* Instead of administering law, the government becomes its own law. This is a subtle distinction, perhaps, but a vital one none the less. In Israel there was no king — no vice-gerent of God (although God had planned a kingdom for Israel foreshadowing the perfect rule of the risen Christ, Deuteronomy 17:14–20) and as a result the people did what was right in their own eyes. The Benjamites, instead of punishing the evil-doers, defended them even to the extent of going to war. The Israelites, on the other hand, took improper oaths and engaged in the genocide of one of their own tribes. The civil powers in Israel, in effect, made war on their own people and they did so to justify their usurpation of the place of the Lord as the lawgiver. Law was now determined by the whim of the dominant party. What most people wanted, or could be persuaded to accept, became the rule. Thus civil power was made omnipotent — it was everything and God's principles were nothing. Such rule is arbitrary and pragmatic rather than God-centred and principled. Arbitrary rule soon gave way to practical anarchy in Israel and the land became ungovernable — except, of course, through terror and anti-scriptural totalitarianism. The very reconstruction of Benjamin is an example of social engineering at its very worst. Does this not speak to our own day? Does our government operate out of the principles of God's Word or from some abstraction such as the 'will of the people', or other arbitrary notions of governmental authority and principles?

Ripe for revival

The wretched state of Israel, and, for that matter, the clear parallels of spiritual and moral declension in our own time, would crush us and cast us down in irreversible despair, were it not for the wonderful paradox of the gospel that Christ came not to save the righteous, but sinners (Matthew 9:13). The apostle Paul says that 'Where sin increased, grace increased all the more' (Romans 5:20). The redemptive-historical significance of the period of the judges becomes apparent. It is that light shall arise in the darkness through the work of a redeemer whom the Lord shall raise up. Israel needs a righteous king. The period of the judges paves the way for David and David himself is a foreshadowing of the Lord Jesus Christ.

It was when Israel was broken and cried out to the Lord that he 'raised up judges who saved them' from their enemies. With righteous zeal we might say that they were 'ripe for judgement', but in the eyes of the Lord they were 'ripe for revival'. We live in a dark day, to be sure. We feel the imminence of divine judgement. We fear the future and we entertain very small hopes indeed for the progress of the gospel. The message for us, if this be our state, is 'Take heart! Be strong and of a good courage! The Lord is working his purpose out! The 'righteous King' is revealed in Christ, who now reigns over all in virtue of his death and resurrection! Look to him! Live in him!' The psalmist stills our hearts when he writes, 'Be still before the Lord and wait patiently for him; do not fret when men succeed in their ways, when they carry out their wicked schemes . . . For evil men will be cut off, but those who hope in the Lord will inherit the land' (Psalm 37:7,9).

'He who testifies to these things says, "Yes, I am coming soon." Amen. Come, Lord Jesus. The grace of the Lord Jesus be with God's people. Amen' (Revelation 22:20,21).

Questions for further study:
1. What is the primary reason for the moral collapse of any society or nation? (Judges 2:13,19.)
2. What was the sin of the men of Gibeah? Was the Levite faultless? Consider what the Bible has to say about homosexuality. What is God's message for so-called 'gay liberation'?
3. What was the duty of the civil authorities of the tribe of Benjamin? What did they do when called to account by Israel? What is the place of God's law in the exercise of civil power? Consider this in relation to our own government and laws (cf. Romans 13:1–7; 1 Peter 2: 13–25).

4. In what ways did Israel make war on their own people? Why did this happen? Why did they suffer such crushing defeats to begin with?
5. Why did Benjamin need wives? How were wives found for them? Was this justified? (Judges 21.)
6. Why were judges raised up by God? What kind of salvation did they effect? What did Israel really need? (Judges 2:16—3:6.) What does Judges 21:25 imply?

4.
The first deliverer

Please read Judges 3:7–11; Joshua 14:6–15; 15:13–19;
Judges 1:11–15

*'But when they cried out to the Lord, he raised up for
them a deliverer, Othniel son of Kenaz, Caleb's younger
brother, who saved them. The Spirit of the Lord came
upon him, so that he became Israel's judge and went to
war'* (Judges 3:9,10).

God's dealings with man are twofold. His ministry is both
for blessing and for curse: the blessings of salvation in a
message that is believed and the curses of condemnation in
a message rejected. This is often overlooked or even rejected
outright in our day. Modern 'gospels' tell men of a better
life in knowing Jesus, but decline to call for repentance
from sin and pervasive reformation of life. Many modern
Christians forget that God's 'negatives' are infinitely positive
as far as his purposes of redemption are concerned. This is
true of his chastisements. In every age God has demon-
strated by fire, pestilence, war and weather his anger with
the wicked. The Bible says that he is 'angry with the wicked
every day' (Psalm 7:11 AV). At the same time his purpose
of saving a people for himself is perfectly served by these
very judgements that he sends abroad in the earth. Why?
Because by these means he tests and prepares the hearts of
men for the reception of the good news of salvation. Thus
he goes on to demonstrate his great love in calling men
back to himself. So it was in that dark day thirty years
after the conquest of Canaan. Joshua and his elders were
dead and the covenant people of God had forgotten him.

Into this situation God brought an oppressor and then, eight years later, a deliverer.

Othniel the deliverer

Othniel was from Judah and was a close relative of Caleb, who was one of the two faithful spies – the other was Joshua – who had brought back a favourable report when Israel had first come to the border of the promised land. Israel did not go in for fear of the Anakim – the 'giants' of the land – and so had to wander for forty years while all the adults except Moses, Joshua and Caleb perished in the wilderness. Othniel was very probably a youth at the time of Caleb's spying mission. He is first mentioned in Joshua 15:17 as the 'son of Kenaz, Caleb's brother'. This could be read either to mean that he was a nephew of Caleb or that he was a half-brother with the same mother but a different father (Caleb was the son of Jephunneh). It could even be possible that he was a full brother of Caleb and that the term 'son of Kenaz' is a general designation of his family group. The ancient Jewish scholars, for textual reasons, favoured this last view. Some modern scholars think that he was probably a half-brother to Caleb. In any event, Othniel was to become Caleb's son-in-law, for he captured Debir from the Anakim – the same people who had scared Israel over forty years before – and won Caleb's daughter Acsah for his wife (Judges 1:11–15). Although Acsah was probably Othniel's niece, such a marriage was not prohibited in the law. All this suggests that Othniel was an important figure in Israel at the time of the conquest. He must have been in vigorous middle age in that period after Joshua's death. Caleb would then have been eighty-five (Joshua 14:10–14) and Othniel in his middle fifties. Thirty years later Othniel would be called of God to do his greatest work.

Israel 'did evil in the eyes of the Lord' (Judges 3:7). They forgot God and served the Baals and the Asherahs. The 'Asherahs' were the sacred groves – specifically the wooden columns that formed the groves – where the Canaanite

goddess Ashtoreth was worshipped. God was angry at this
backsliding and he gave them into the hands of a Syrian
king who was appropriately named Cushan-Rishathaim –
'Cushan of the double wickedness'. This was probably
the Israelite name for him, needless to say. His kingdom
was in Mesopotamia, for 'Aram Naharaim' means Syria of
the two rivers – the land between the Tigris and the
Euphrates. For eight years Israel suffered his depredations
until 'they cried out to the Lord' (3:9). Israel's faithful
cried out. Israel was at the end of its own resources. The
'arm of flesh' had failed, as it always will, and now, in total
helplessness, they were ready to be blessed. So the Lord
heard them and raised up that old warrior of a former
generation, the victor of Debir, the conqueror of the Anakim.
He received the Spirit of the Lord and went to war. And
we are told with majestic simplicity that the Syrians were
defeated and 'so the land had peace for forty years'. Othniel
probably judged Israel for only a few of these years. Unlike
our English translation, the Hebrew does not imply that he
lived for the whole forty years. The legacy of Othniel was a
generation of peace in Israel. This, then, is the story. What
are we to learn from it for our own day?

Revival is the Lord's doing

There are three principal points of application for the church
of God in our time and these are expressed in three striking
phrases in the passage we are examining.
1. *'He raised up for them a deliverer'* (3:9b). Othniel did not
just happen along. It was no mere coincidence that there
was a fine courageous, vigorous and steadfast old soldier
down in Judah who just fell into the job of rescuing Israel
from the Syrians. The truth is that, appearances and the
speculations of historians to the contrary, nothing ever
works that way in history, for the simple reason that God
is working out in time his eternal purpose. This is the pre-
supposition which must underlie, and which alone can give
real meaning to, the study of history. Othniel, like a Kutusov,

a Blücher, a Hindenburg or a MacArthur, was called in old
age to lead his country's army. It is clear that God raised
him up for a specific redemptive work in the life of his
people. When we realize this, we then begin to see the
significance of Othniel's earlier life as preparation for his
greatest task. The covenant child in Egypt, the witness of
God's mighty hand at the Red Sea, the participant in the
wilderness wanderings, who saw both the backsliding of
Israel and the faithfulness of the Lord, and the conqueror
of the Anakim, now became Israel's first judge and deliverer.

The implication for us is clear. If we see the church backslidden and, consequently, under chastisement from the
Lord — and who can deny that is true of the professing
church today? — then we must not seek our own solutions
or lean on 'the arm of flesh', but rather turn to the Lord
for his deliverance. Ultimately we are pointed to Christ,
who is *the* Deliverer, and it is in and through him that we
must seek the 'men for the hour' as far as the leadership
of the church and the ministry of the gospel is concerned.
Christ is all! He is the only Saviour! To whom shall we go?
He has the words of eternal life!

2. *'The Spirit of the Lord came upon him'* (3:10a). Whatever his preparation in the course of life or his natural
capacities and his gifts and graces, Othniel was specially
endowed for this task. He was anointed by the Holy Spirit
in a special measure.

This recalls to us the words of Isaiah (61:1,2) which
Jesus applied to himself in his address in the Nazareth
synagogue: 'The Spirit of the Lord is upon me, because
he has anointed me to preach good news to the poor. He
has sent me to proclaim freedom for the prisoners and
recovery of sight for the blind, to release the oppressed,
to proclaim the year of the Lord's favour' (Luke 4:18,19).

It is because of this special endowment of the Holy
Spirit and his subsequent triumph over sin and death that
Jesus has won for his people a salvation in which believers
have the promise of the presence of that same blessed third
person of the Trinity, the Holy Spirit, in their hearts. Both
Othniel's endowment with the Holy Spirit and the 'salvation'

he effected for Israel were very limited in scope when compared with the work of the Saviour of the world. The principle is the same and comes to its full expression in the risen Christ.

Should we not then pray that the Lord would pour out his Spirit upon us? Should we not pray for him to raise up 'men for the hour' — for our time — men after his own heart (Jer. 3:15) — who will lead his people in this present darkness in the so-called Christian West? Should we not desire that the Lord endow his people with the presence and gifts of the Holy Spirit for the great tasks facing the body of Christ in these days? More pointedly, do you want the Holy Spirit to fill you and be powerfully active in your heart? Do you really desire to have him do 'immeasurably more' than all you can 'ask or imagine, according to his power' that is at work within you? (Ephesians 3:20.) Are you yearning for such transformation in your life and in the church of Christ? This is of the essence of true spiritual growth and of revival in the church.

3. *'They cried out to the Lord'* (3:9a). This phrase appears before the others, but is mentioned last simply that it may be the more emphatically impressed upon our consciousness. This is where all spiritual growth and all revival begins. We really begin to live in Christ when we are brought to see, by faith, that we are helpless to save ourselves and even to increase our faith or our devotion to him. Crying out to the Lord is the *sine qua non* of the renewal of true comfort, true peace and true joy in the Christian life and in the life of the church as a whole. God chastised his people with Syrian oppression until they began really to pray. 'Before I was afflicted,' says the psalmist, 'I went astray' (Psalm 119:67).

Very often when we are faced with terrible troubles (they may be personal or they may consist in fears about the times in which we live) we do cry — but not to the Lord. We look at our sorrows and woes, to our feelings about the injustices around us. We cry — over spilt milk, in self-pity — when we should be crying to the Lord. 'They cried to the Lord in their trouble', said the psalmist, 'and he delivered them from their distress' (Psalm 107:6,13,19, 28). God's message here is 'Cry to the Lord! Lay your troubles at the foot of the throne of grace! He will hear you! He will deliver you! He will give you peace! He has promised this in his Word! The salvation you will know, because Christ has died and risen in victory over sin and death, is so much more than that which Israel was to receive in the day of the judges. Yet Othniel the deliverer points to Christ the Deliverer. We need a Saviour and he is the Lord Jesus Christ, who will in no way cast out those who come to him. 'Come to me, all you who are weary and burdened, and I will give you rest.'

Questions for further study:
1. What were the 'Asherah'? Review the nature of Canaanite religion (consult a good Bible encyclopedia). Why was the Lord so angry at his people? Do you think God is angry with the professing church ('Christendom') today? If so, why?
2. Review Joshua 15:13–19 and Judges 1:11–15 and see what you can find out about Othniel. What clues to his character can you find in these passages?
3. What is recorded as qualifying Othniel for his task? (Judges 3:7–11.) Apply this to the church in our day.
4. Why do 'oppressions' come to the Lord's people? In what way does this shed light on disasters, wars, famines and all forms of oppression in our day? What is the 'finger of God'? (Exodus 8:19.) How might a Russian believer use, and find blessing in, such biblical teaching? Consider Psalm 107 and Psalm 119:67.
5. When God points his 'finger', what is to be man's first response? What is the implication of this for, say, poverty in a Hindu country *and* for the responsibility of the Christian church in relation to such a land?
6. Consider the endowment of the Holy Spirit in the light of Luke 4:18–21 and such passages as John 14–16, the Acts of the Apostles and 1 Corinthians 14.
7. What is the great practical point of all obedience to the Lord? (Judges 3:11.) Why is there so much restlessness today?

5.
A pointed message

Please read Judges 3:12–31

'Ehud then approached him while he was sitting alone in the upper room of his summer palace and said, "I have a message from God for you"' (Judges 3:20).

The story of Ehud is the stuff of which swashbuckling Hollywood movies used to be made. It is an earthy tale; it has drama, daring and death in full measure and, of course, it has a happy ending — for the Lord's people. Then there is always that well-worn joke about Ehud being a 'sinister' character — 'sinister' being the Latin word for 'left-handed', which personal characteristic Ehud certainly used to good effect. It is not for our entertainment, however, that we are told this story, but rather for our encouragement to trust unequivocally in the promises of God. As with all the judges, there is certain focus upon spiritual revival in the midst of terrible moral and spiritual decline.

To put this present episode in perspective, we must review the general course of events in Israel since the conquest. Israel invaded Canaan around 1406 B.C. and the conquest was completed in seven years. Joshua died around 1390 B.C. and less than a quarter of a century later Othniel was raised up to defeat the Syrians (1367 B.C.). The land had peace for forty years, until 1327 B.C. Because of renewed backsliding Israel was oppressed by the Moabites for eighteen years until, in 1309 B.C., the Lord raised up Ehud to deliver his people. Israel would celebrate 100 years in the promised land in the third year of Ehud's judgeship, yet in that short time there had been two great national backslidings,

twenty-six years of foreign occupation and two great deliverances. The turmoil of these times must have made a vivid
impression upon the people. What is so striking — and
sadly so — is that God's mighty works of deliverance
apparently made little impression upon the generation
arising after each particular period of revival. This is not
merely some ancient phenomenon. In the history of
Christ's church one can cite many instances of this same
pattern. Thus the spiritual revival of the seventeenth century in Scotland gave way to the sterile moderatism of
the eighteenth century. This in turn was swept away in
the evangelical resurgence of the mid-nineteenth century,
only for that to be eclipsed by the now dominant, though
dying, liberalism and modernism. And even now we appear
to be witnessing the beginnings of a fresh wind of the Holy
Spirit as a new and serious evangelical faith gathers disciples
across the country and gains increasing influence in the
counsels of churches long given up for dead.

Ehud's destruction of Moab

The essential facts are as follows. For eighteen years, Eglon,
the King of Moab, held sway over Israel. The humiliation
of that nation was underlined by the fact that Eglon's headquarters had been established in the City of Palms, which
was Jericho. Now Jericho had been the symbol of Israel's
victory over the enemies of the Lord since Joshua had
destroyed it a century before. In fact, Joshua had pronounced an oath to the effect that anyone who rebuilt
Jericho would incur the anger of the Lord (Joshua 6:26).
Eglon was soon to learn that this was no idle threat, but
in the meantime, Israel suffered for its sins under this
heathen's yoke.
    God's people cried out to the Lord and the Lord gave a
deliverer in the person of Ehud of Benjamin. Although not
specifically stated to be a judge, it is clear enough that this
is what he was. He was also left-handed. Taking advantage
of these two factors — his position as a leader of Israel

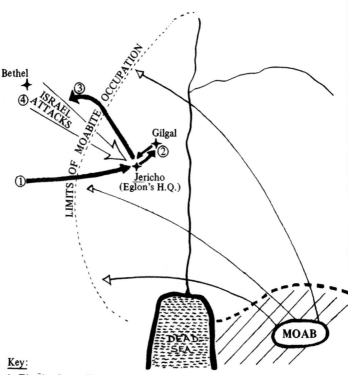

Map 2 — Ehud's victory over Moab

Bethel

③

④ ISRAEL ATTACKS

LIMITS OF MOABITE OCCUPATION

Gilgal

②

①

Jericho
(Eglon's H.Q.)

DEAD SEA

MOAB

Key:
1. Ehud takes tribute
   to Eglon
2. Ehud to Gilgal —
   Doubles back to Jericho
   Assassinates Eglon
3. Ehud escapes to raise
   Israel's army
4. Israel attacks Moab and
   destroys her power

and his left-handedness — he soon devised a plan to rid Israel of Moabite oppression. As a leader, Ehud would bear the annual tribute to his suzerain, King Eglon. As a left-handed man, he would be able to kill Eglon, even while his right hand, raised in salute, would assure the king that there was no danger. Our modern practice of shaking hands with the right hand is just one way of indicating that one comes in peace, for the usual sword-arm is extended in greeting, empty of a weapon. By means of this stratagem, Ehud believed he could execute God's judgement upon the wicked Eglon.

The tribute was delivered to Eglon without incident. No doubt Ehud, who I believe was being led by the Lord in his actions, wanted to impress Eglon as a loyal and harmless vassal. The Israelite party left for Gilgal where it seems that the Moabites had put up some stone idols, presumably to reinforce their superiority over Israel's God, whose power in bringing Israel across the Jordan had been memorialized with a cairn of twelve stones. There, too, Israel had renewed the covenant with God and had seen the revival of the covenant sign of circumcision. Ehud turned back alone from Gilgal and sought an audience with Eglon. Truthfully he declared that he had a 'secret message' for him. The king's retainers were dismissed. Then Ehud revealed that his message was 'from God' — also absolutely truthful. The king rose from his throne, presumably out of respect for a divine message, and so unwittingly presented Ehud with the perfect target. Ehud's secret message from God was instantly revealed. The sword flashed as it was plunged into the king's midriff and Eglon crashed to the floor and died. Ehud escaped through the porch, rallied his men and destroyed the Moabites in battle, thus gaining eighty years of peace for Israel.

A message from God

If there is a unifying theme in this story, apart from the general theme of the whole book, namely, revival out of declension, it is contained in words in verse 20: 'I have a message from God for you.' There are at least three aspects to this theme of communication from God to men.

1. *'The Lord gave Eglon king of Moab power over Israel'* (3:12). The Moabites, assisted by two other Transjordanic peoples, the Ammonites and the Amalekites, were given free reign by God to oppress Israel. To us these nations just seem to be tongue-twisting names from the distant past — names, to be sure, of peoples who gave God's people a hard time, but 'names' all the same, not very significant in themselves. We correctly see that this lengthier period of oppression teaches us a basic principle of all corrective punishment, namely, that if we do not get the message from lighter afflictions, then God will send us heavier afflictions until we do. But we still miss the point of the names of these tribes.

To Israel there would have been great significance in these particular oppressors. These three nations were, you see, rather closely related to God's people and, furthermore, all three owed their origin to the backslidings of God's covenant people! Moab and Ammon, according to Genesis 19:30–38, were the sons of Lot's wicked daughters through incest with their father, whom they contrived to get drunk for that precise purpose! So began two of the most godless peoples ever to live on this earth! The other point of this triangle of depravity, Amalek, was descended from Esau, the reprobate line of Abraham's seed (Genesis 36:9–12). So great was the Amalekite hatred for Israel that the Lord decreed its extinction as a race (Deuteronomy 25:17–19). So, to the discerning Israelite, it was a case of the sins of the past returning to scourge the sins of the present. The warning to us is one of repentance. Repent and return to the Lord, or otherwise your sins will certainly find you out. 'Get rid of the old yeast, that you may be a new batch without yeast — as you really are', said the apostle Paul, 'For Christ, our Passover Lamb, has been sacrificed . . .' (1 Corinthians 5:7). The message of God in the oppressions of Israel is one of repentance and faith and so, in terms of the New Testament, is a charge to flee to the Redeemer, even Christ, who alone is able to save us from our sins.

2. There is also a message for the enemies of the Lord. *'There they saw their lord fallen to the floor dead'* (3:25). If Israel had been wicked, then Eglon had been worse. Israel was called to repentance, but God's message for Eglon was one of final judgement and condemnation. The question is always raised as to whether Ehud was not simply an assassin or a murderer. If this were so, it might tend to blunt somewhat the cutting edge of this event as God's judgement. The text surely points us to the conclusion that it was indeed a divinely mandated execution of judgement, in which Ehud acted in obedience to the special revelation of God. Ehud was raised up for this task of deliverance and proceeded to execute it in that perfect blending of the sovereign providence of God and his own skill and courage which is recorded in the passage. We ought always to remember that there is no precedent here for assassinating anyone in the name of God, however monstrous a tyrant such a person might be. We have no right to 'do evil that good may come'. When God specially commissions a man to execute his judgements, we can only stand in awe at his dealings. One commentator remarks that for us in the New Testament age there is a final word from Jesus on the use of the 'sword' to defend the Lord's cause and kingdom. When Peter took his sword to the high priest's servant in Gethsemane, Jesus said, 'Put your sword back in its place, for all who draw the sword will die by the sword' (Matthew 26:52). The message for us in this is that the church of Jesus Christ must not bear the sword. Individual Christians have no warrant to emulate Peter in Gethsemane (John 18:10,11). On the other side, the message to the Eglons of the world is simple: the Lord will surely bring the wicked to judgement, whatever his means in any given age. Ultimately the Lord Jesus Christ shall return to judge the living and the dead. Meanwhile let the Lord's people patiently await his appearing.

3. *'The land had peace for eighty years'* (3:30). The Lord has a message of encouragement for us in these words.

The Hebrew word for peace is *shălôm*. This is not the mere absence of war or civil unrest. It is rather a state of covenant blessedness. God blesses the life of his believing people with temporal and spiritual prosperity, and they live before him in righteousness according to his revealed will. He speaks *shălôm* to his people (Psalm 85:8. *cf.* Numbers 6:24–26).

Years later, Isaiah would tell Israel, 'O my people who live in Zion, do not be afraid of the Assyrians, who beat you with a rod and lift up a club against you, as Egypt did. Very soon my anger against you will end and my wrath will be directed to their destruction . . . In that day their burden will be lifted from your shoulders, their yoke from your neck' (Isaiah 10:24,25,27).

A very few verses later, the prophet goes on to give the reason for this relief: 'A shoot will come up from the stump of Jesse; from his roots a branch will bear fruit. The Spirit of the Lord will rest upon him – the Spirit of wisdom and of understanding, the Spirit of counsel and of power, the Spirit of knowledge and the fear of the Lord – and he will delight in the fear of the Lord' (Isaiah 11:1–3).

Once again we are pointed to the Lord Jesus Christ, the 'righteous Branch' (Jeremiah 23:5). Again deliverance for Israel so long ago points us to the cross of Christ. There Christ Jesus 'pulled' the sting of death; there he won peace for ever for all his people. 'Come to me, all you who are weary and burdened, and I will give you rest.' 'There remains, then, a Sabbath-rest for the people of God . . . Let us, therefore, make every effort to enter that rest, so that no one will fall by following their example of disobedience' (Matthew 11:28; Hebrews 4:9,11). He is the 'Prince of Peace' (Isaiah 9:6) – the Lord of our *shălôm*.

Questions for further study:
1. Why was Israel oppressed for eighteen years by the Moabites, over against the eight-year oppression of Cushan-Rishathaim? What principle of corrective punishment is taught here?

2. What was the significance of the oppression by the Moabites, Ammonites and Amalekites? (Genesis 19: 30–37; 36:9–12.)
3. Why did Eglon rebuild Jericho for his headquarters? (Joshua 6:26.) What was the meaning of the idols at Gilgal? (Joshua 4:19–5:9.) What was God's purpose in this?
4. Consider Ehud's stratagem. What evidence is there in the text to support the view that he was led by God to execute divine justice? Is this a precedent for New Testament age Christians to follow? Explain.
5. How does God execute his judgements in the world?
6. In the light of Isaiah 10:34–11:10, what is the message to the Lord's people who are suffering under afflictions? What does this tell us about the task of the church in the world?

6.
A mother in Israel

Please read Judges 4,5

*'Village life in Israel ceased, ceased until I, Deborah,
arose, arose a mother in Israel'* (Judges 5:7).
*'So may all your enemies perish, O Lord! But may they
who love you be like the sun when it rises in its strength'*
(Judges 5:31).

'The prosperity of fools shall destroy them,' says the writer
of the Proverbs (1:32 AV). The eighty years of peace in
Israel after Ehud's destruction of the Moabites should have
seen the firm establishment of Israel in the ways of the Lord.
Yet we are told that in the days of Shamgar, whose judgeship was probably towards the end of that period, there was
awful degeneration in Israel, so that the Lord gave them
over to the oppression of the Canaanites under Jabin, King
of Hazor (who is not the Jabin of Joshua 11:1) and his
military commander, Sisera. During this terrible time of
oppression there was a breakdown of normal life such that
Deborah could testify, 'Village life in Israel ceased, ceased
until I, Deborah, arose, arose a mother in Israel' (Judges
5:6,7). The northern part of Israel fell under the Canaanite
hegemony for twenty years (1229–1209 B.C.) and this was
the longest and fiercest occupation to which God's people
hitherto had been subjected. Sisera, we are told, 'cruelly
oppressed' Israel with his apparently first-class army which
possessed no fewer than 'nine hundred iron chariots'. After
twenty years of misery, Israel was brought to her knees and
'cried out to the Lord for help' (4:1–3). The Lord heard
their cry and raised up a remarkable woman, the prophetess
Deborah, to deliver his people from the Canaanites (4:4).

48

Deborah the prophetess

The narrative may be resolved into four distinct sections. First is the account of Deborah's organization of Israelite resistance to Jabin and Sisera (4:4—11). Secondly, we are told of Israel's victory at 'Taanach by the waters of Megiddo' (4:12—16). Third is the death of Sisera at the hands of Jael (4:17—24) and finally there is the song of Deborah, in which the whole panorama of deliverance is celebrated before the Lord (5:1—31).

1. *Deborah's call for Israel to resist* (4:4—11). Deborah is remarkable for three main reasons: she had the gift of prophecy, she was a judge in Israel and (obviously but significantly) she was a woman. She was the first prophet to arise in Israel since the time of Moses. She was the first and only woman ever to exercise civil authority in Israel at the calling of God. In that song she wrote under the inspiration of the Holy Spirit, she called herself a 'mother in Israel' — an expression which surely captures the essence of this unique woman and her unique calling to be God's appointed leader in what was very much a 'man's world' at that time. To say she was a 'mother in Israel' is to say that she was a spiritual mother to the Lord's people, whom she guided and nurtured by means of the oracular gift with which the Lord had endowed her. Just as kings were to be 'fathers' to their people, so Deborah, because she was a woman and a leader, is called a 'mother in Israel'. The essence of this encomium is in her relationship to her God. She was above all a believer in the Lord and a labourer in his vineyard. How grotesque it was some years ago to see this beautiful description, redolent as it is of personal godliness, applied to the otherwise eminent, but atheistic humanist, leader of modern Israel, Golda Meir! Deborah defies identification with women in later ages who rose to political leadership, whether Golda Meir, Indira Ghandi, or Margaret Thatcher or even Joan of Arc. Deborah stands alone as a woman called of God to exercise a redemptive purpose in his plan for his people's salvation. This is the essential and fundamental point of her judgeship and if we do not grasp

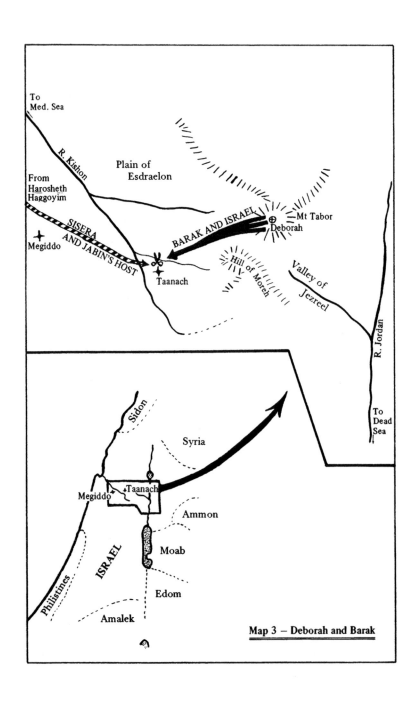

Map 3 — Deborah and Barak

this, then we can only misunderstand and misapply the lessons of this amazing episode in the life of God's people.

It was to Deborah — prophetess and judge — that God revealed his will that she should send for Barak of Naphtali to raise an army of 10,000 men to fight Sisera, and it was also to Deborah that he revealed his strategy for the victory of Israel. Two particular features of these verses call for careful attention.

In the first place, let us notice the brilliant strategy unfolded by Deborah (4:6,7). Barak and his army had no heavy weapons (5:8), whereas Sisera had his professionals and his chariots. To get round this difficulty, the Israelites would occupy Mt Tabor at the head of the Kishon valley (also called the plain of Esdraelon — see map). Miles down the valley, not far from the Mediterranean Sea, lay Sisera's base, Harosheth Haggoyim. This dominated the plain and gave Sisera the capacity to deploy his highly mobile army very swiftly in answer to any threat from the Israelites. This was precisely the design of Deborah. Sisera would advance inland across the plain, while Barak would remain invulnerable on Mt Tabor until the Lord's moment for victory should arrive. When the Lord brought flash-floods down the otherwise diminutive Kishon, thereby destroying the effectiveness of Sisera's chariots, the Canaanites were simply blown away by the Israelite onslaught (5:20,21).

Secondly, we must notice the significance of Barak's unwillingness to take the field without the presence of Deborah (4:8,9). Since there is no indication of hesitation on Barak's part to answer the original call to arms and every evidence that he was a courageous and accomplished warrior, it would be quite unwarranted to ascribe motives of cowardice to him. It is clear, however, that he suffered from a certain lack of faith, since he attempted to place a condition on his future obedience to the Lord. Deborah did not demur, however, but, in agreeing to go with the army, did tell Barak that the honour of dealing with Sisera would not be his, but would belong to a woman. To prepare us for this eventuality, the writer records in verse 11 the fact that a Kenite clan from the Negev far to the south

had settled near Sisera's stronghold. The Kenites were kins-
folk of Moses. It was to Jael, the wife of Heber the Kenite,
that the honour of dispatching Sisera would accrue in due
time.

2. *Barak's victory* (4:12—16). Later Deborah and Barak
would sing, 'From the heavens the stars fought, from their
courses they fought against Sisera. The river Kishon swept
them away . . .' (5:20,21). It is evident from this highly
poetic language that God timed a great storm to intervene
decisively for his people. The near-dry Kishon became a
torrent, the plain became flooded and the chariots were set
in disarray (5:22). This did not make Israel's victory easy,
but it did give her lightly armed tribal levies the tactical
edge they needed to defeat Sisera's modern army. Just as
Sisera's assets — the chariots — were rendered liabilities by
water and mud, so Israel's liability — lack of heavy weapons—
became a positive asset. Now the mobility and the momentum was with Israel. The result was a great triumph
(4:14—16). 'All the troops of Sisera fell by the sword; not
a man was left.' This not inconsiderable honour fell to the
worthy Barak.

3. *The death of Sisera* (4:17—24). Sisera, providentially
spared from death at the hands of Barak, met his nemesis
on what he believed to be friendly territory. He stumbled
into the camp of Heber the Kenite and sought refuge in
the tent of Jael, his wife. We are not told why he went to
her tent. We are not told what he was thinking as she gave
him milk to drink and a bed in which to sleep. As to her
motive for driving the tent-peg through the head of the
sleeping Sisera, we are left in darkness, but we do know
that the Lord, through the prophetess Deborah, hailed Jael
as the 'most blessed of women' (5:24). Sisera carried out
the will of the Lord — unknowingly — in oppressing Israel,
but perished in his sins. Jael evidently carried out the will
of the Lord in dispatching Sisera to a lost eternity and God
declared her 'blessed'. For us there is a great mystery, but
the Judge of all the earth does right (Genesis 18:25) and,
to the eye of faith, there is a most solemnizing example of
the perfect accomplishment of his sovereign will.

4. *The song of Deborah* (5:1–31). This song, composed under the inspiration of the Holy Spirit, is a review of God's mighty deeds in delivering Israel. It is analogous to the song of Moses (Exodus 15), which praises God for Israel's deliverance from Egypt. Deborah's song, as we have seen, supplies some details which are not mentioned in the narrative passage. We might briefly note the structure of the song.

Introduction (5:2–11). This outlines the general course of events which led to the battle at Taanach.

I. *The summons to Israel* (5:12–18) details which tribes came to fight and which did not. Compare this also with verse 23, where Meroz is cursed for failing to come.

II. *The battle at Taanach* (5:19–27) is recounted together with the melancholy tale of Sisera's end.

III. *The expectations of the enemy* (5:28–30) are solemnly recorded, in particular the experience of Sisera's mother.

Conclusion (5:31). Deborah prays for the vindication of God's cause and the future blessing of the people of God.

The victory brought peace to Israel for forty years. When Deborah and Barak sang in celebration of God's redemption of Israel, the people of God had been brought to a new beginning. They were indeed beginning to be 'like the sun when it rises in its strength'.

'May they who love you be like the sun'

There can be no question that these words from verse 31 express the theme of Deborah's judgeship. This is true in perhaps two ways: firstly, with respect to the indication given by her life of the glorious place of women in God's economy – she was 'a mother in Israel' – and secondly, in regard to the glory of God's people as the chosen light of God in a dark world.

1. *'A mother in Israel'* (5:7). Deborah is one of a number of prophetesses raised up by the Lord to serve Israel. Others include Miriam (Exodus 15:20), Huldah (2 Kings 22:14), and Isaiah's wife (Isaiah 8:3). Deborah alone is called to exercise authority in Israel as a judge. These facts have a positive and a negative application.

Positively, they indicate the glorious place of women in the economy of God. The idea of inherent inferiority of women to men is completely dispelled by the life of Deborah. Her prophetic gift and her judge's authority cannot be said to argue for the ordination of women in the New Testament church or for modern ideas of 'fifty-fifty' marriages, where the man is not the head of the woman — the New Testament Scriptures are explicit on these subjects. There is, however, a certain light shed upon the place of women and it is this: whatever may, in the wisdom of God, be *denied* to women under the gospel (authority in the church, ordination to the gospel ministry, headship in the family), it is not denied because of any inherent inferiority. It is rather for the proper balance of responsibilities, for the proper ordering of the family and of the church, in order that God might be glorified by effective service and witness in each area.

Negatively, there is an implication that Deborah's very standing as a judge is a divine rebuke to the supine male 'leadership' in Israel (which was, in fact, non-existent). This comes out in the fact that Barak's hesitancy to go to Mt Tabor without the prophetess resulted in the honour of killing Sisera going, not to some other *man*, but to a *woman*. This was a definite reproach for Barak and the men of Israel, notwithstanding the fact that they would (properly) be the actual combatants in the battle with Sisera's host. There is, then, a call to God's *men* to fulfil their full responsibilities for leadership before the Lord.

2. *'May they . . . be like the sun'* (5:31). Deborah's prayer is for God's people to shine as light in the world. This involves at least three aspects. First of all, is the exaltation of God's people as the source of light and truth in the world. It is glorious to belong to God and to see his victories over

sin in one's life. This is nothing less than exaltation. Secondly, the people of God are to be the bearers of light to others in the Stygian darkness of a fallen world. Christ sent the church to preach the gospel. If the church fails to do so, then no one will hear and no one will be saved. Of course, the Bible makes clear that the Lord will have his witnesses till the end of time, but the encouragement to us is equally clear — if we do not bear the light to the nations, no one else will. So we must be faithful to the Lord! Thirdly, and pre-eminently, the Lord's people are to bring glory to the Lord. They are to be an adornment. They are 'precious jewels' that glitter in his crown. They point to Christ. Indeed, Christ is the Light, the true light that, coming into the world, enlightens every man, the light of life — *the* Light. This is the glorious conclusion and promise of the message of that great lady, Deborah the prophetess.

Questions for further study:
1. What is particularly humiliating to Israel in this third oppression? (Joshua 11:1–11; Judges 4:1–3; 5:6–8.)
2. What is unique about Deborah? What does it mean to be a 'mother in Israel'? Is it proper to apply such an epithet to Golda Meir? If not, why not? (4:4–7; 5:6,7.)
3. Consider Barak's relationship to Deborah. What is the significance of Deborah's prophetic statement in regard to the honour for Sisera's death going to a woman? Why couldn't it have gone to another man? (4:8–10.)
4. Consider the relationship of faith and responsibility (and of the mighty deeds of God and man's exercise of means) in relation to the strategy and tactics of the Israelite victory at Taanach (4:6–8, 14–16; 5:19–22.)
5. Was Jael justified in killing Sisera? (4:17–24; 5:24–27.)
6. Review the song of Deborah (5:31). Can you find parallels in Scripture? What is its theme? Can you apply this to yourself?

7.
Jehovah-Shalom

Please read Judges 6

'When Gideon realized that it was the angel of the Lord, he exclaimed, "Ah, Sovereign Lord! I have seen the angel of the Lord face to face!" But the Lord said to him, "Peace! Do not be afraid. You are not going to die." So Gideon built an altar to the Lord there and called it "The Lord is Peace"' (Judges 6:22–24).

Three times in two and a half centuries, Israel had fallen into the most fearful idolatry and wickedness. Three times the Lord had chastised them by permitting their enemies to oppress them. Three times they had cried out to the Lord for help and three times he had raised up judges who would deliver them. These judges, Othniel, Ehud and Deborah, were God's instruments of temporal and spiritual revival and 'as long as the judge lived' God 'saved them out of the hands of their enemies' (2:18). It seems that when the judge died the people rapidly returned to their wicked ways. So it was that for the fourth time since entering Canaan, Israel fell away from righteousness and God chastened them for seven years by permitting the Midianites and other nomadic peoples from the east to ravage the country. They naturally chose to invade the land around harvest time. In an agrarian economy this is the only sensible time for pillage. The produce of the land was the real wealth of Israel and it is not surprising that seven years of Midianite depredation reduced Israel to dreadful poverty. It was in this desperate condition that they cried to the Lord for help. Once again the Lord raised up a new judge to be their deliverer. He was

Gideon, son of Joash, of the Abiezrites of the tribe of Manasseh.

The preparation of Gideon

The story of Gideon is a long one and deserves more attention than can be given to it in one study. This chapter, therefore, will consider only Gideon's preparation for his battle with the Midianites. The battle itself and its aftermath will be treated separately in a succeeding chapter.

The sixth chapter of Judges consists of four distinct sections, each covering one phase of the development of both the situation in Israel and the progress of Gideon from relative obscurity to national leadership.

The first section (6:1—10) recounts *Israel's cry for help and the initial response of the Lord.* Why Israel cried to the Lord has already been noted. This closely parallels the earlier oppressions which Israel experienced. There is one difference in this present case and it is very significant. In the former cases the Lord raised up a judge directly upon hearing Israel's cry for help. This time the Lord delayed raising up a judge and first sent an unnamed prophet who preached a message which was designed to convict the people of their sin. He reminded them of their covenant heritage and rebuked them for departing from it. Evidently the purpose was to bring the people to repentance, which, as we shall see later, is not the same thing as crying for help, even if the crying is to the Lord.

In the second section (6:11—23) *the Angel of the Lord appears to Gideon and calls him to save Israel.* It is the appearance of the Angel of the Lord that is the most significant event in the whole episode. The Angel had appeared once before, at Bokim, where the people of God were denounced for their faithlessness and the scene was set for the recurrent pattern of sin and salvation that pervades the period of the judges (2:1—5). He was none other than the eternal Son of God, the Logos or Word (John 1:1) in his pre-incarnate state, appearing in human form as a foretaste of his taking our nature so many centuries later. The Lord found Gideon at Ophrah, a village in the Valley of Jezreel only a few miles from the place where, a century before, Barak had defeated Sisera. Gideon was threshing his wheat in a winepress to avoid detection by the Midianites. In this slightly less than heroic posture the Lord hailed him: 'The Lord is with you, mighty warrior!' (6:11,12.) Gideon certainly felt the epithet undeserved, although, in reality, it was his commission from God. He demurred (6:13). The Lord restated the commission, but Gideon remained hesitant: 'How can I save Israel? My clan is the weakest in Manasseh' (6:14,15). For a third time, but with greater emphasis, the Lord reiterated his point: '*I* will be with you, and you will strike down the Midianites.'

At this point, it appears to have dawned on Gideon that his visitor might be from God and so he asked for a sign that would prove this. He prepared meat and unleavened bread and broth, presumably for a meal for his guest. It was not to be, however, for the Angel of the Lord had him pour out the broth on the ground and put the meat and bread on a rock, whereupon he touched it with his staff and it was consumed by fire, just as the first sacrifice in the tabernacle had been some three centuries earlier (Leviticus 9:24). The Angel then disappeared! Gideon now realized who this 'man' really was and he began to fear for his life for he had seen him 'face to face' and knew that no man shall see God and live (Exodus 33:20). The Lord immediately reassured him, 'Peace! Do not be afraid. You are not going to die' (6:17–24). The acceptance of the food offering indicated the acceptance of Gideon, and Gideon was enough of a theologian to know that!

The third part of Gideon's preparation was in the form of *a test from the Lord* — a test of faith by which the Lord would both prove Gideon's mettle and his own faithfulness (6:25–32). We can surely identify with Gideon's hesitancy, but we can only marvel at his faith. It is true that he carried out God's will at night, for fear of his family and neighbours, but carry out God's will is what he did. How sweet a confirmation of the Lord's pleasure it must have been when his father stood with him against the hostile crowd and even gave him a new name, Jerub-Baal, 'Let Baal contend'! This name, in its own way, preaches that same message of the psalmist when he penned the ninety-sixth psalm:

> For all the gods are idols dumb,
>   which blinded nations fear,
> but our God is the Lord, by whom
>   the heavens created were
>
> (Psalm 96:5, metrical version).

In the final division of the chapter we find *Gideon,* now the acknowledged leader of Israel, *gathering an army to fight the hosts of Midian* (6:33–40). For a second time, Gideon asked for a sign which would confirm the promise that Israel would be saved by his hand (6:36). This is highly suspicious. He had already received two amazing confirmations of this, one in the very presence of the Angel of the Lord. Gideon knew the truth as well as anyone to whom God revealed his will, whether by theophanic appearance (as with the 'burning bush' or the Angel), miraculous sign, spoken Word, or the plain text of the Scripture. Was he hesitant because he wanted an 'out'? Naturally he was trembling before the enormity of his task and, in his fears, like Jonah in relation to Nineveh, he would rather be elsewhere. Hence his insistence on another sign — that sign which has given the English language the expression 'to hang out a fleece'. Gideon put his fleece on the ground and asked God to bring dew on it, while leaving the ground dry. God did this, but Gideon wanted more 'proof' and asked for the reverse. God duly performed this also and the silence of the text as to Gideon's reaction testifies to the fact that he had nothing left to do but obey the Lord. The Lord had closed any door of escape.

Jehovah-Shalom — 'The Lord is Peace'

Surely the confession of Gideon made in the building of

the memorial altar at Ophrah, namely 'The Lord is Peace'
(6:24), is the overarching theme of the Lord's calling and
preparation of Gideon. Everything points to the patience,
or longsuffering, of God. Perhaps three particular events
evidence this quality most markedly.

The sending of the prophet (6:7–10) is a testimony to
the fact that when Israel cried to the Lord for help, it was
not in the spirit of true repentance for sin. The world is
always crying for help, but few in it are concerned about
sin, repentance and the necessity of reconciliation with
the living God. The prophet's ministry at one and the same
time shows the inadequacy of Israel's response and the
mercy of the Lord in having listened to her anyway. It is
this latter aspect that is most impressive. The Lord does
not stand on ceremony. He does not insist on a fully correct
manner of approach, before he will listen to them. No! He
loves the unlovable. He seeks the lost. He 'winks' at their
ignorance (Acts 17:30 AV). He deals with them with their
pain and their confusion and their mixed motives, and he
deals with them in grace. Once I was on a trip to Turkey.
My friend and I had our cameras stolen and sought to report
this to the police and secure an affidavit that we had done
so, in order to make an insurance claim once we got home
to Britain. The Turkish police refused to take a report,
claiming that we had sold them and wanted to collect the
insurance as well. So we went to the British Consulate in
Istanbul to lodge our complaint. The official at the desk, to
whom we blurted out our story, refused to listen to us
until we said, 'Good morning' — after his third stony 'Good
morning' we got the message! The Lord does not wait for the
'Good morning'. He works out his purpose and gets to the
heart of the real problem. Christians can stand on ceremony
so easily. We want our 'rights'. We want the proper 'form'.
We insist on the other fellow forgiving us before we forgive
him. The Lord shows us what the way of true grace really
is and Gideon later on, in 8:1–3, shows that he learned the
lesson well.

The Lord also shows his patience in *the way he dealt with
Gideon's repeated calls for 'signs'* that would prove that it

was really God who was telling Gideon what to do. Gideon
was afraid, but he was presumptuous in testing the Lord in
this way. True faith looks beyond fear, even though it
continues to experience its distracting power. The Lord,
however, dealt with him as he found him — a weak, wavering saint. The Lord gave him the signs and pacified his
troubled heart. We ought not to reason from this that God
approves of 'hanging out a fleece' as a proper method of
finding his will. The use of the 'means of grace', in
particular the Word of God and prayer, are to be distinguished from seeking a 'sign'. Neither is the discerning of
providential circumstances in the light of the principles
of the Word the same thing as 'hanging out a fleece'. Sometimes Christians use prayer and 'circumstances' as if they
were a 'fleece' and treat their conclusions as if they were
miraculous special revelations from God. Some Christians
talk (promiscuously) in terms such as 'The Lord spoke to
me,' 'God told me to do this,' and the like. Sometimes it
works in reverse — as in Gideon's case — where the object
of the exercise is to get out of doing God's will, precisely
because we know exactly what the Lord wants. This person
says, 'I'll pray about it,' knowing full well that it is a delay-
ing tactic, not a means of speedier obedience. But, oh,
how gracious the Lord is to his children! He comes over
our weaknesses and our provocations to bless us beyond
our imaginings. So it was with Gideon. So it is with all
who belong to Christ.

Perhaps the most striking feature of Gideon's experience
is *his ordinariness.* He seems an unlikely leader. He seems
very much to be one of us. He was hesitant. He had little
evident ambition. He had almost to be dragged into the
job by the Lord. Surely this is a testimony, all the more,
to the patience and the mercy of God. We are encouraged
to open our own eyes to wider vistas of service to the Lord.
Let us recall that it was the Son of God who dealt with
Gideon — the same Son who took our nature and was born
of the virgin Mary in that Bethlehem stable. Perhaps,
Christian friend, you, like the publican in Luke 18, cannot
lift your eyes to heaven. You are gripped by a sense of sin,

a sense of unworthiness, perhaps even of relative uselessness to the Lord. Then lift up your eyes and look upon Jesus Christ and in him, through faith in him, be encouraged by the witness of Gideon, who 'by faith . . . subdued kingdoms' for God. Christ is our King. He has subdued the kingdom of darkness. We shall be more than conquerors through him who loved us.

Questions for further study:
1. What was the nature of the Midianite oppression? Was it worse than earlier oppressions? If so, cite reasons in the text.
2. What is the significance of the Lord's sending a prophet to Israel? (6:1—10.) Does this indicate something about Israel's response to God's chastisements?
3. What did the Angel of the Lord look like? Why was Gideon uncertain as to his visitor's identity? Who was the Angel of the Lord? (Gen. 16:13; 32:30; Exodus 33:20.)
4. How did the Angel of the Lord convince Gideon of his identity? What does this tell us about:
   a. the Lord, *b.* the Christian life?
5. What is the significance of the fire consuming Gideon's food offering?
6. Why was Gideon called Jerub-Baal? Consider the meaning and implications of the altar of Baal.
7. Consider the sign of the 'fleece' in relation to guidance. Apply to the present time.
8. How does the Lord deal with sinners? Why is God called Jehovah-Shalom?

8.
The Lord will rule!

Please read Judges 6:1–8:35

'The Israelites said to Gideon, "Rule over us — you, your son and your grandson — because you have saved us out of the hand of Midian." But Gideon told them, "I will not rule over you, nor will my son rule over you. The Lord will rule over you"' (Judges 8:22,23).

In the previous study of Judges 6, we saw how the Lord called Gideon to lead Israel against the Midianites. The army of Israel, drawn from the tribes of Asher, Manasseh, Naphtali and Zebulon, was already gathering when Gideon hung out his fleece and called upon the Lord to prove by miraculous signs that he, Gideon, would truly be the instrument of Israel's salvation. This seeking of signs from God is certainly no precedent for us to follow; it was presumptuous of Gideon to test God in this way and it is all the more presumptuous of the modern Christian to 'bargain' with God. We have the completed canon of Scripture, the indwelling of the Holy Spirit in the hearts and minds of believers and the Christ-instructed pastoral ministry of the church. Gideon, for all that he lived in a time of the incomplete revelation of God's plan of redemption, nevertheless had been given a complete revelation of God's will as to his leadership of Israel. Gideon was faltering when he insisted on the 'fleece'. The Lord graciously granted his requests, none the less, and thereby reinforced the very confession of Gideon that he is *'Jehovah-Shalom'*, 'The Lord is peace.' God's love is a love that will not let his servants go and the Lord, in giving the requested signs, shut off any way of escape that Gideon might have desired. Now he had to face his task as Israel's judge. The moment of truth had arrived for Gideon.

A sword for the Lord

The two chapters which record the battle and its aftermath, Judges 7 and 8, may conveniently be divided into four sections, each covering a distinct phase in Gideon's progress.

Israel's preparation for battle is the subject of Judges 7:1–15. This consists of two parts. The first, verses 1–8, is concerned with manpower, while the second, verses 9–15, focuses upon morale – specifically, the encouragement of Gideon.

After Gideon's double test of God with the fleece, the reduction of Israel's army from 32,000 to 300 constituted a double test of Gideon and his men. Even with all her men, Israel was outnumbered by a ratio of more than four to one – the Midianites had 135,000 – yet now the Lord reduced the army to three companies of infantry – a reduction of over 99%. This was necessary, the Lord told Gideon, so that Israel would not be able to boast that they saved themselves (7:2). The first test was a test of faith. All those who were afraid were excused and soon 22,000 men left the camp (7:3). The second test was a test of works. The remaining 10,000 were to drink from a stream: those who got down on their knees and lapped with their tongues were to be rejected and only those who 'lapped with their hands to their mouths' were to be retained. Only 300 adopted this watchful posture and these, the Lord declared, would be the means of deliverance (7:7). These were the men with the necessary abilities, as well as steadfast faith.

If Gideon had secret doubts as to the prospects for his 'army', the Lord certainly dispelled them with his next ploy. He told Gideon that if he was afraid to attack, he should go to the Midianite camp. There he should listen to

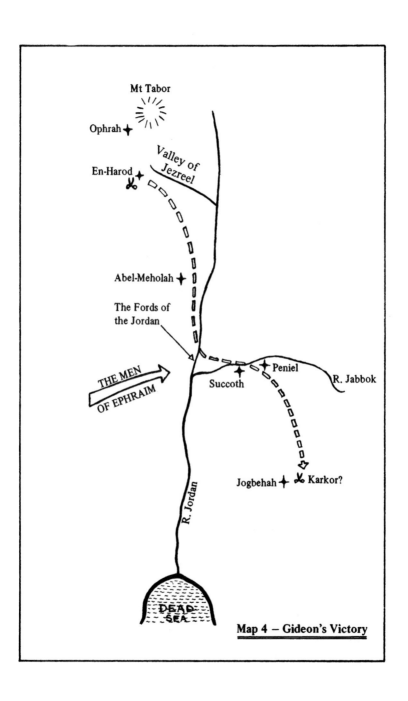

Map 4 – Gideon's Victory

what his enemies were saying. Then he would be encouraged to attack. Gideon took advantage of this invitation and went down to the camp. There he heard one Midianite tell a friend of his dream. In the dream, a barley loaf had fallen into the camp and knocked down a tent. 'Ah!' said the friend, 'That can only be the sword of Gideon. God has given the Midianites and the whole camp into his hands.' The exultant Gideon, no doubt convinced of the value of good intelligence-gathering, praised the Lord and, returning to his camp, prepared to lead his men into battle (7:9–15).

The battle, recounted in Judges 7:16–22, was not so much a battle as a psychological stratagem, pure and simple. If the Midianite's dream had wide currency among his compatriots, then the defeatist spirit must have rendered them as ripe for a rout as that same dream had filled Gideon with a thirst for victory. Each Israelite had a trumpet and a pitcher with a torch inside. Around 10 p.m., when the 'middle watch' would have begun, they moved into position (the three watches were 6 p.m.–10 p.m., 10 p.m.–2 a.m., 2 a.m.–6 a.m.). At the appointed signal they blew their trumpets, smashed their pitchers, waved their torches and shouted their battle-cry: 'A sword for the Lord and for Gideon' (7:20). The result was total confusion in the Midianite camp. They milled around in a panic, flailing at each other in the dark and soon a great tide of frightened men and beasts washed down the valley of Jezreel to the Jordan. Through the night they fled towards Abel-Meholah, running the gauntlet of God's wrath for thirty miles — and this was just the beginning!

The pursuit must have continued for two days or more. Judges 7:23–8:21 recall the multifarious events which took place in that hectic time. Gideon needed all the help he could muster, so he called back the men who had not been selected by the Lord the day before and he sent runners south to Ephraim to ask that tribe to seize the fords of the Jordan (see map). The slaughter was terrible. From En-harod in the valley of Jezreel to Jogbehah (near modern Amman, Jordan), a distance of some seventy miles, the roads and tracks were littered with the offal of war.

120,000 Midianites fell, according to Judges 8:20. The last organized force — 15,000 men under their kings, Zeba and Zalmunna — went down to defeat on the battlefield at Karkor (8:10–12). Zeba and Zalmunna were subsequently put to death by Gideon, on account of the fact that they had killed his brothers (8:18–21).

What is perhaps of greater significance than even the 'mopping up' of the Midianites in this pursuit is the way in which Gideon had to face and deal with opposition from certain of the people of God. Two specific problems arose.

The first problem came from the Ephraimites. This tribe had answered Gideon's call with great zeal and effectiveness (7:24,25). They were, nevertheless, quite dissatisfied with Gideon because he had not called them to the fight at En-harod. 'They criticized him sharply' (8:1) and as is so often the case with self-centred criticism, they made no effort to inquire as to his reasons, far less understand them. Had they done so in a right spirit, they would have been told that it was the will of the Lord and that Gideon had no liberty to call them or employ anyone other than the three hundred. Proud Ephraim appears to have had no such interest. Like the Macdonalds who marched off the field before the Battle of Culloden because Prince Charles Edward Stuart did not give them the place of honour at the right of the line,[1] the Ephraimites were deeply offended because they had not been called to a place of honour on the field of En-harod. Gideon's response is a splendid implementation of the proverbial maxim: 'A gentle answer turns away wrath' (Proverbs 15:1). Gideon was in the right and Ephraim was in the wrong. If ever there were an open and shut case, this was it, but did Gideon stand up for his rights? No! He did not seek personal vindication. He perceived that, their sinful pride notwithstanding, Ephraim was eager to fight for the Lord and so he simply disarmed their contentious spirit by commending their real contribution to the cause. 'At this, their resentment against him subsided,' says the chronicler (8:3). Oh, that we might learn this same spirit in our dealings with contentious brethren! Gideon knew that personal attacks on him were neither here nor there;

as far as his personal vindication was concerned, let it be in the hands of the Lord. Meanwhile he must marshall these Ephraimites in the work of God!

The second problem Gideon had to face was his double rejection by the people of Succoth and Peniel, two cities of Israel situated on the Jabbok river, the boundary between Manasseh and Gad (8:4–21). At both places Gideon asked for food for his men — a not unreasonable request from one's head of government in time of war, but one contemptuously rejected by both cities. Gideon vowed to deal with them when he returned in triumph with the kings they were so afraid of in his custody. In due course, he did return and exacted the promised penalties of these two cities (8:13–17). The immediate question is 'Why the severity with Succoth and Peniel and the generosity with the men of Ephraim?' The answer is, surely, that although the Ephraimites were quite wrong in their criticism of Gideon, they were committed to the Lord's cause, whereas the people at Succoth and Peniel refused to make any such commitment and therefore committed acts of treason against God and his people. Gideon acted judicially with Succoth and Peniel because it was in fact a civil crime against the theocratic government, while he acted judiciously with Ephraim because their essential loyalty to God was not vitiated by their personal attacks upon him.

The final portion of the narrative deals with the consequences of the destruction of the Midianites (8:22–35). The people had a new hero and desired to establish a hereditary monarchy with Gideon as the founder of the dynasty. He declined with that magnificent declaration — and implied rebuke — 'The Lord shall reign over you.' It is one thing for the Lord to *give* a king to his people, but for his people to *make* someone their king is spiritual revolution. For this reason, many of Israel's kings were to be a disaster, while David was to be the man of God's choosing and, of course, the forerunner of Christ Jesus, the King of kings and Lord of lords. The Lord did bless Israel while Gideon lived: 'The land enjoyed peace for forty years' (8:28,33).

For all that, there were, once again, ominous signs of cracks in the fabric of the covenanted nation. Two points deserve particular attention. Gideon requested and received some seventeen hundred shekels of gold — approximately 688 ounces — from the plunder of the Midianites. This he had fashioned into an ephod, which was the garment used by the high priest in seeking the will of God (Exodus 28: 6–30; 1 Samuel 23:6,9). There is no evidence that Gideon meant this to supplant the ephod of the priests at Shiloh. It was probably only to be a memorial to the great deliverance that God had given them. Like all human memorials, and more than most of them, this golden ephod was liable to become an object of veneration to the superstitious. This is in fact what happened. It even became a snare to Gideon and his family, which presumably means that in some way he used it or usurped a priestly role (8:27). The second indication of Gideon's weakening and a change in Israel's thinking is the evidence of a kingly style of living on Gideon's part. This too must be seen in the light of the people's invitation to him to assume the kingship. Gideon accumulated wives and concubines — itself quite contrary to God's Word (Deuteronomy 17:17) — and assumed the style, if not the title, of an oriental monarch. Good man that he undoubtedly was, Gideon was not immune to the evils of the day. The Lord was with him all his days and he died 'at a good old age' and was buried at Ophrah.

The Lord is King

If there is a common thread throughout this story, it is surely expressed in Gideon's great declaration: 'The Lord will rule over you' (8:23). Whatever authority he may have had — and it was real, as the men of Peniel and Succoth discovered — Gideon realized that he was really a servant. He led the people, but under a sovereign God. At every stage, Gideon appears to have been very much aware of this perspective. In the preparation for the battle, Gideon submitted at every point to God's leading. In the battle itself, it was 'a sword for the Lord' first and 'for Gideon' only secondarily. In his gentleness with Ephraim and his severity with Succoth and Peniel, it was his service of the Lord and the Lord's sovereign rule which moulded his actions. Gideon did not do what was right in his own eyes. He stood forth in contradiction of the spirit of his age and graces the pages of God's Holy Word as a glorious example of what God can do with the 'weak things of the world'. His is an abiding memorial to saving faith in the Lord (Hebrews 11:32).

There is, too, a watchword for every believer in the words of Judges 8:4 . . . Gideon and his faithful followers were 'exhausted yet keeping up pursuit'. Gideon was no Greek hero. He was no 'superstar'. He was one of God's 'weak things' raised up to 'confound the mighty'. Of course, he and his men were fit and clearly in vigorous health, but a pursuit of a night and a day will make even such men exhausted. The point is that they were persevering in the face of every difficulty. They were spending themselves for their Lord and he was renewing their strength by his grace. Here is the calling of every child of God. When the Lord rules over you, you have no greater desire than to give yourselves for him, even Christ Jesus your Saviour.

> The Lord is king indeed! Let peoples quail and fear!
> He sits above the cherubim; let earth be moved!
> The Lord in Zion rules, and over all is high;
> O praise his great and dreadful name, the Holy One!
> Psalm 99:1−3 (metrical version)

Questions for further study:
1. Why did the Lord reduce Gideon's army so drastically? What was the significance of the 'double trial' involved in this reduction?
2. Was the Lord also preparing the Midianites for the battle? What does the encouragement that the Lord gave Gideon tell us about this?

3. How was the battle conducted? Consider Gideon's overall strategy.
4. Consider Gideon's response to the criticisms levelled by Ephraim. Contrast this with his treatment of Succoth and Peniel. What does this teach us about our dealings with other professing Christians? (8:1–3.)
5. What did the people want in regard to the civil government? What was Gideon's response? Consider the implications for us today (8:22–24.)
6. What was Gideon's first major error after his victory over Midian? Consider the application of this for us today (8:25–27.)
7. What was Gideon's second mistake and how did it bear evil fruit? (8:29–9:6.)
8. What is the central thrust of the account of Gideon's judgeship? (Hebrews 11:32.)

Reference
1. 1746. The last battle on British soil, in which the second Jacobite rebellion was crushed and the Catholic Pretenders to the British throne (the Stuarts) were denied their claims for ever.

9.
A thorny problem

Please read Judges 8:29–10:5

*'Finally all the trees said to the thorn-bush, "Come and
be our king." The thorn-bush said to the trees, "If you
really want to anoint me king over you, come and take
refuge in my shade; but if not, then let fire come out
of the thorn-bush and consume the cedars of
Lebanon!"'*   (Judges 9:14,15.)

The final words of Judges 8 give an ominous sense of in-
completeness to the account of the revival under Gideon.
Israel, we are told, 'failed to show gratitude to the family
of Jerub-Baal (that is, Gideon) for all the good things he
had done for them'. What that failure to show gratitude
meant in practical terms is soon revealed, for the ninth
chapter of Judges records what happened to the sons of
Gideon. It is an ugly story of murder and conspiracy over
which arches the wrath of God against sin. In the process,
the family of Gideon vanished from the stage of history
and again a new judge, named Tola, was raised up to save
Israel, not from a foreign oppressor, but from herself. Israel
could well have said, in the words of a character from a
modern American cartoon series, 'We have met the enemy,
and he is us!'

It is clear that a number of factors alluded to in the
account of Gideon's life as a judge came to produce their
evil fruit only after that good man's death. Shakespeare
was acutely perceptive when he wrote, 'The evil that men
do lives after them; the good is oft interred with their
bones.' This was certainly the case with Gideon with respect

to Israel's history in the three years immediately following his death. In the first place, Gideon's kingly life-style had not been consistent with his refusal of the kingship and it is clear enough that the desire of the people for a king, other than the Lord, had not abated. This was to result in the ready acceptance of the usurper Abimelech as king. In the second place, the immorality of Gideon in accumulating a harem and raising seventy-one sons made for an unhealthy intra-dynastic struggle. The fact that it was the one illegitimate son, Abimelech, who was the most ambitious is hardly surprising; the bastard sons of princes have always made the best usurpers! In the third place, the return of Israel to false religion, helped along by Gideon's golden ephod, removed the theological and spiritual barriers to making a king and, indeed, provided the very means of carrying out Abimelech's scheme! (9:4.) This would not be the last time in world history that organized religion financed revolution and terrorism!

The rise and fall of Abimelech

The ninth chapter of Judges records five distinct phases in the disastrous career of Abimelech. These may be outlined as follows:
1. Abimelech kills his brothers and gains the crown (9:1–6).
2. Jotham, his only surviving brother, foretells Abimelech's fall in a parable (9:7–21).
3. Abimelech quarrels with the Shechemites (9:22–29).
4. The Shechemites are utterly destroyed by Abimelech (9:30–49).
5. Abimelech meets his own end at Thebez (9:50–57).

The Lord then restores blessing to Israel by raising up Tola and Jair as judges over his people. This is recorded in Judges 10:1–5.

Abimelech gained his kingdom by sheer murder (9:1–6). The method adopted has been standard practice in oriental despotisms for millennia. Until relatively recently the Sultans

of Turkey were required to kill all their brothers in order to
secure the throne. Thanks to polygamy this was equivalent
to wiping out a small town! The same method is practised
by all dictatorships, of course, whether oriental or occi-
dental, monarchic, fascist or communist. With the support
of his relatives in Shechem and money from the Temple
of Baal-Berith, he put out a contract on his brothers in
Ophrah. All except Jotham were killed — apparently in
the fashion of a public execution ('on one stone', 9:5) —
and Abimelech was crowned king in Shechem 'beside the
great tree at the pillar' where nearly three hundred years
earlier God had renewed his covenant with Joshua and
Israel (Joshua 24).

Jotham, who had escaped death at Ophrah, now turned up
at Shechem — or rather on the slope of Mount Gerizim,
from which he could address Abimelech in relative safety.
There he delivered a remarkable address which turned out
to be prophetic (9:7–21). This address is often called a
parable, but in reality it is a fable. It does not deal with
the kingdom of God and it is not a story drawn from real
life; therefore it is a different genre from that of the biblical
parable. This fable recounts how the trees set about electing
a king. The trees asked the olive tree, the fig tree and the
vine — the three great fruit-bearing trees of the east — in
turn, to be their king. Each refused, not wishing to give
up his fruitfulness for this dubious honour. At length, the
trees turned to the useless thorn-bush and he was only
too ready to be their king, although he accepted with a
dire warning: 'If you really want me to be king, come and
take refuge in my shade; but if not, then let fire come out
of the thorn-bush and consume the cedars of Lebanon!'
(9:15.) The application is obvious: the people (i.e. the
trees) had asked Gideon (the fruitful tree) if he would
be king, but he had declined, so now they turned to
Abimelech (the worthless thorn-bush) and he was eager
to take it. The time was coming when the people of
Shechem would no longer want Abimelech for their king
and so fire from Abimelech would consume them. Jotham
expressed an additional hope, namely, that fire would go
out from Shechem and consume Abimelech (9:20).

It was not too long before Abimelech's world started to come apart. After three years the people of Shechem rebelled against his authority (9:22–29). 'God did this,' we are told, 'in order that the crime against Jerub-Baal's seventy sons . . . might be avenged' (9:24). A soldier of fortune named Gaal (pronounced Gah-al) arrived at Shechem and, having won over the people, incited them to open rebellion.

The governor, Zebul, was still loyal to Abimelech and he informed his king of what was going on, thus setting in motion a chain of events which would lead to the utter destruction of Shechem (9:30–49). On Zebul's advice, Abimelech approached Shechem secretly by night. At sunrise they emerged from hiding and advanced on the city. Gaal and Zebul, who was evidently playing along with the Shechemites while still being secretly loyal to Abimelech, saw this from the city gate and Zebul urged Gaal to go out and fight (9:38). This he did and he was duly defeated and chased back to the city. Abimelech retired to Arumah, while Zebul, still acting as if loyal to the Shechemites, took the opportunity to remove Gaal, who was no doubt discredited by his defeat. The Shechemites thereby lost their competent leadership. Some time later, Abimelech surprised the people at Shechem as they went out to work in the fields, seized the city, destroyed it and sowed it with salt, an act symbolic of the desire that the city be as barren as a salt desert (9:45). The town's elite, meanwhile, had ensconced themselves in the citadel, called 'Beth Millo' in 9:20 and 'the stronghold of the temple of El-Berith' in 9:46. This Abimelech burned down, thereby killing the last thousand surviving Shechemites. What happened to the double-dealing Zebul we are not told.

Abimelech then turned his attention to a nearby city, named Thebez, which apparently had been implicated in Shechem's rebellion (9:50–57). He got into the city, but the people had all moved into the citadel. It was there, while trying to burn it down, that he met his end. He was felled by a millstone dropped on him by a woman and to avoid the stigma of being killed by a woman he ordered his armour-bearer to run him through with his sword. 'Thus

God repaid the wickedness that Abimelech had done to his
father by murdering his seventy brothers,' is the laconic
epitaph in Judges 9:56.

The curse of Jotham had been fulfilled to the letter
and the 'thorn-bush' was 'a thorny problem' no more!

Wickedness has a price

The ninth chapter of Judges is not an easy one to apply to
our own day. There is no specifically redemptive theme
in it, as in the accounts of the judges that we have studied
up to this point.

It is possible, of course, to glean some moral lessons from
the story. For instance, there is the interesting fact that in
Jotham's fable when the trees look for a king, the best trees
decline because they do not wish to give up their present
usefulness, and in the end the post has to go to a worthless
thorn-bush. Perhaps this tells something about politics,
politicians and the electorate! It has nothing to do with
political systems, but it does tell us something about
ambition. As the godly Charles Simeon put it, 'Worthless
men affect [i.e. desire] the honours which the wise and
good decline.' Gideon, the man of God, was content to
decline what the evil Abimelech lusted after. This is a general
truth for every age. 'Study rather to be good than great,'
said Simeon. Be ready to enter into any task or office to
which the Lord calls you – in politics, business, the church
or whatever. What is of the essence is knowing the Lord
and therefore knowing yourself in the light of the Word
of God.

The pervasive theme, however, is that wickedness has a
price-tag and that the Lord will see to it that his righteousness is fully vindicated. Gideon's seventy sons were gone.
Whatever God did to Abimelech and Shechem would not
bring them back, but true justice fundamentally is retri-
butive. The penalty is paid. That is the way it will be in
the great judgement when Christ returns. All unpaid
accounts will be met in full. Oh, that those who are happy

to do without Christ might be convinced of this! The psalmist observed that many godless people had long comfortable lives and apparently had easy deaths (Psalm 73:4,5). This caused him to wonder if there really was much use in being a follower of God's righteousness. It seemed to him that it was believers who had a hard time, while the careless godless sinners had a wonderful life, full of fun and unhindered by scriptural controls and limitations (Psalm 73:3–14). He knew he was wrong to think this way, but it confused him until he 'entered the sanctuary of God'. 'Then,' he says, 'I understood their final destiny. Surely you place them on slippery ground; you cast them down to ruin. How suddenly they are destroyed, completely swept away by terrors!' (Psalm 73:18,19.) He then goes on to renew his trust in the Lord. It is significant that it is 'in the sanctuary of God' that the psalmist sees the destiny of the wicked. There, in the tabernacle, atonement was made for sin and there were placed the symbols of the covenant of grace – and all this in the very presence of God. The reality of God's righteousness is plainly evident in his presence, in the symbols of a covenant of grace and in the necessary sacrifices for sin. Unbreakable righteousness requires atonement for sin. The atonement is the gospel – good news of a way of salvation where the price is paid by the Redeemer for those who could never pay for their sins. Therefore, for those who reject the salvation offered in this gospel, there is nothing but awful retribution – eternal condemnation in which the supposed securities and pleasures of this life will cease even to be a memory in the endless night of the lost!

A redemptive note

We are not simply left on this sombre note, however, for Judges 10:1–5 properly belongs to the period of Abimelech. Tola and Jair were called to be judges over Israel. It is possible that they judged Israel at the same time – verse three says that Jair 'followed' Tola, but that probably means only that he assumed his office after Tola assumed his (and not after Tola had died). Tola is said to have 'saved' Israel. From whom? Surely from the evils of the reign of Abimelech! Chaos and civil war had been used by God to chastise his people, and still he sent deliverance to them.

God saves just as surely as he obliterates wickedness. The Lord Jesus will return to judge the living and the dead. His seal is upon his own people; their sins are covered; their hearts are quiet as they contemplate their great High Priest; the hope of heaven becomes an eternal reality; their joy is in the presence of the Lord for evermore.

Questions for further study:
1. Review the background to Abimelech's desire for a crown and the Shechemites' eagerness to finance his quest (8:30—9:6.)
2. Consider Jotham's 'parable'. What did it mean? What general principles does it teach? (9:7—21.)
3. Why was it a sin for Israel to make a king for herself?
4. Review the subsequent history of Shechem and Abimelech (9:22—57.) How was Jotham's curse fulfilled?
5. From what did Tola (and Jair) save Israel? (10:1—5.)
6. What are the major points of application for us today in the passage we have studied? (8:30—10:5.)

10.
Watch your words!

Please read Judges 10:6–12:7

'Then the Spirit of the Lord came upon Jephthah. He crossed Gilead and Manasseh, passed through Mizpah of Gilead, and from there he advanced against the Ammonites. And Jephthah made a vow to the Lord: "If you give the Ammonites into my hands, whatever comes out of the door of my house to meet me when I return in triumph from the Ammonites will be the Lord's, and I will sacrifice it as a burnt offering"'

(Judges 11:29–31).

Jephthah, like all of God's servants in this fallen world, is a flawed trophy of grace. Like the wicked Abimelech, he had an illegitimate birth, was an outcast from the home of his father and brothers and yet came to rule over Israel. In contrast to Abimelech, however, he was called by God to deliver his people and was a man of faith upon whom the Spirit of God came in great power. In spite of this and his status in God's plan of redemption, as recorded in Hebrews 11:32, Jephthah is remembered most as the man who made a rash vow before the Lord, which was to have painful consequences for himself and his family. This should touch our hearts in the same way as Gideon's timorousness and David's backslidings, for in the sins of the saints we see the frailty that clings to all of us in this life, even to those Christians who evidence notable growth in personal godliness, and we are reminded of something that we do not often like to admit, namely, that there is a potential within believers for such rash actions and wicked deeds. It will not do to look

79

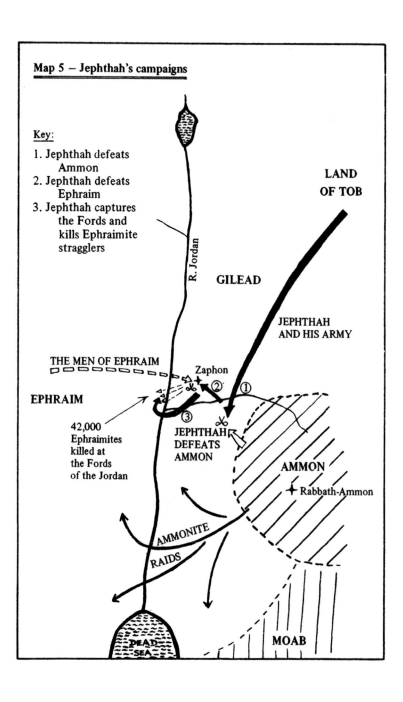

Map 5 — Jephthah's campaigns

Key:

1. Jephthah defeats Ammon
2. Jephthah defeats Ephraim
3. Jephthah captures the Fords and kills Ephraimite stragglers

LAND OF TOB

R. Jordan

GILEAD

JEPHTHAH AND HIS ARMY

THE MEN OF EPHRAIM

Zaphon

② ①

EPHRAIM

42,000 Ephraimites killed at the Fords of the Jordan

③

JEPHTHAH DEFEATS AMMON

AMMON

✦ Rabbath-Ammon

AMMONITE RAIDS

MOAB

DEAD SEA

upon Jephthah with an attitude of imagined superiority, as if we were immune to his weaknesses. The attitude should rather be one of compassionate sympathy, as of those who, like that good man, know how much they need the power of the Holy Spirit to keep them from falling and to present them faultless before the presence of God with great joy.

A mighty warrior

There is, as the Preacher said, 'nothing new under the sun' (Eccles. 1:9). Israel turned to false gods once again and the Lord sent the heathen Ammonites and Philistines to oppress her. This lasted for eighteen years and apparently it was the former nation that was his chief instrument, for it was among the Gileadites — the tribes of Gad and Manasseh—that the brunt of it was felt.

What is of special significance in this account is the Lord's emphasis upon the necessity of a true repentance on Israel's part. The Israelites eventually cried for help and confessed that they had sinned (10:10). This did not satisfy the Lord, who reminded them that he had delivered them repeatedly in the past, but this had not prevented them from returning to their false gods and their immorality. 'Go and cry out to the gods you have chosen,' said God. 'Let them save you when you are in trouble!' (10:14.) This challenge brought forth a real change. It has been said truly that repentance is not only *for* sin, but *from* sin. Israel had to do more than be sorry; the idols had to go! They had to return to the Lord and cast themselves upon his mercy. Then the Lord would deliver them. Indeed, the Scripture says that he 'could bear Israel's misery no longer' (10:16). Such is the nature of the matchless love of God for his covenant people.

Israel needed a leader and so the Lord raised up Jephthah, a Gileadite of the tribe of Manasseh, to fight the Ammonites (11:1–11). This man, because of the hatred of his brothers, had been living to the north in the 'land of Tob' and, as so often happens when men are put through hard experiences, he evidently developed notable skills as a survivor and a leader, for it was to him that the elders of Gilead were led to turn when they needed a general for the army. There is invariably an ironic twist even to the movements of God's free grace. This is true of the Lord Jesus Christ: 'The stone the builders rejected has become the capstone.' The unwanted bastard, Jephthah, had to be sought, *as God's man,* for the generalship of the armies of Israel! When God sheds his grace upon men, the very experience reminds them that it is real grace — unmerited, unearned, undeserved and unlooked for as far as human wisdom is concerned. Grace blesses through humbling. The elders of Gilead had to swallow their pride as part of receiving that blessing. This is always true in the realm of God's gifts. The elders were apparently as sincerely humbled as they were desperate for a leader and Jephthah, for his part, accepted with appropriate graciousness. This was confirmed before the Lord in Mizpah.

War followed immediately (11:12—40). At first, Jephthah attempted to negotiate, but in the end was obliged to appeal to the contest of the battlefield. Ammon would not withdraw without a fight. Israel fought and the Ammonites were utterly defeated. The general pattern is similar to that of previous deliverances. The unique feature of this particular episode is the vow which Jephthah took prior to the campaign (11:30,31). This vow was to bring a great deal of grief to Jephthah and his daughter and it has been the subject of controversy to biblical interpreters in the millennia that separate us from that great warrior (11:34—40).

Jephthah's vow

There are basically two schools of thought on Jephthah's vow. One believes that Jephthah actually put his daughter to death by sacrifice, while the other believes that his vow only involved consecrating her to perpetual virginity as an attendant at the tabernacle at Shiloh (cf. Exodus 38:8; Judges 21:20,21; 1 Samuel 2:22). The former view was favoured by the older Jewish commentators and the early church fathers as well as many later eminent commentators, such as Matthew Henry. A recent popular treatment of Judges takes the same position.[1] In the last few hundred years this has been questioned and it has been suggested that the evidence of the text points not to the daughter's immolation, but only to her consecration to the exclusive service of the Lord. I believe that the preponderance of the evidence is for the second view. Although it is not possible to give a thorough treatment of the subject in this brief study, it is necessary to understand the main reasons and these will be discussed in a moment.

What must be understood at the outset is that Jephthah's vow, whatever its implications for his daughter, was a foolish vow; first, because it was not required by God; second, because it was in the nature of bargaining with him — 'Win my battle, Lord, and I'll do this . . .'; and third, because it was presumptuous in that it promised the consecration of anything or anyone, without explicit regard to the specific rights, privileges and circumstances of those who could be affected by it — it was open-ended and thoughtless, when any vow ought to be specific and carefully considered. Many a Christian has done the same kind of thing and the warning of this passage is pointedly relevant to Christian experience today. How many men have said to the Lord, 'Lord, if you get me out of this tight spot, I'll give the rest of my life to you as a preacher'? How many go into the ministry, or waste years going to seminary and seeking a call to a church unsuccessfully, because of a rash vow? Does God save us because of our promises? Of course he doesn't! Yet it is true that whole lives can be misdirected by this kind of misconception. Never bargain with God; rather, receive his revealed will as set forth in the Bible and trust in his free and sovereign grace to keep you and to bless you!

To return to the original question: why do I believe that Jephthah's vow involved consecration rather than death by sacrifice for his daughter? In the vow itself the crucial words are 'and I will sacrifice it as a burnt offering' (11:31).[2] From the straightforward reading of these verses, it would seem that only death could be the daughter's fate. There

was, however, a deeply rooted idea in Israel of 'meta-
phorical sacrifice of persons to Jehovah'.[3] The first-born
of Israel were consecrated to the Lord, but they could be
and were in fact redeemed (Numbers 3:12,13). The Levites,
in Numbers 8:10—16, were consecrated to the Lord by the
laying on of hands of the children of Israel, just as they
would other sacrifices. The Levites, in turn, substituted for
themselves two bullocks, upon which they laid their hands
as they consecrated them to the Lord as a burnt offering.
This same general idea finds expression in Leviticus 27,
where provision is made for the substitution of a ransom
in money for persons who were consecrated to the Lord
(Leviticus 27:2—13). Jephthah could have invoked this
provision to release his daughter. The fact that he did not
is an indication, surely, that, for all his grief that it had to
be his daughter who was consecrated, this consecration was
not in the nature of sin in itself, as would be the case were
she to be put to death (cf. Exodus 20:13; Deuteronomy
12:31). The text does not appear to demand that Jephthah's
oath necessitated the death of the one who would first come
to greet him on his return.

This is confirmed in the actual execution of the vow.
Jephthah's daughter gently acquiesces and there is no
mention of death. In fact, only perpetual virginity is ever
mentioned and that three times (11:37,38,39). She asks
for two months to mourn her loss of the potential to marry—
an indication of the sorrow with which childlessness was
viewed in Israel. Children were God's heritage in Israel.
They were a man's true wealth. Jephthah allows her this
time and then carries out the vow. Is it not significant that
the last word on the daughter herself is 'And she was a
virgin'? The final verse (11:40) then recalls that each year
the young would 'commemorate' her, presumably at Shiloh.
The word rendered 'commemorate' in 11:40 appears only
in Judges in the song of Deborah (5:11) where it is rendered
'recite'. The idea is not so much the commemoration of a
sad event, as the reciting of something God has done.
Jephthah's daughter was willing that her father's vow be
honoured. Why? Because the Lord had avenged him of his

enemies, the Ammonites (11:36). While she lived and as long as she was remembered in Israel, the triumph of the Lord was remembered.

The Lord turned the foolish vow of Jephthah into a glorious memorial to his saving grace, through the lovely submissiveness and self-sacrifice of a godly daughter.

The accents of rebellion

Ephraim was a restless tribe. They had objected to Gideon's failure to call them to En-harod to fight the Midianites. Now they rose in rebellion against Jephthah's rule, claiming, falsely, that they had not been called to fight against Ammon. The result was civil war (12:1—6). The Gileadites defeated Ephraim in battle and captured the fords of the Jordan. There they applied a simple test to everyone who sought to cross. If anyone denied he was from Ephraim he was asked to say the word 'shibboleth', which means either 'a flood of waters' or 'an ear of corn'. The point was that the pronunciation of the word betrayed the origin of the speaker. The Ephraimites could not say 'sh' so that '*sh*ibboleth' came out as '*s*ibboleth' — in just the same way as the Scottish Highlanders of today can be distinguished from Lowland Scots by their pronunciation of 'worship' as 'worsip'. This little distinction was to cost 42,000 men their lives and to give the world a byword for the finest point of detail in ethics — the shibboleth, the finest point of doctrine or practice, held to with intensity of passion appropriate to matters of life or death. The original 'shibboleth' at the fords of the Jordan was, indeed, a matter of life or death. It was the occasion of God's chastisement of this most rebellious tribe. Later the psalmist would comment on the emerging pattern of Ephraimite opposition to the Lord:

The men of Ephraim, though armed with bows,
    turned back on the day of battle,
they did not keep God's covenant
    and refused to live by his law.
They forgot what he had done,
    the wonders he had shown them.

(Psalm 78:9–11).

Only when this opposition was crushed did peace come
to Israel under the judgeship of Jephthah (12:7).

Man's words and God's Word

The general theme of Judges, namely, renewal by divine
grace after a period of backsliding, is once more evident,
but, as with each earlier episode, we are able to discern a
unique applicatory theme. There is a recurrent focus in the
story of Jephthah upon man's words in relation to the will
of God.

Even an otherwise wholly innocent feature of a regional
accent was used by God to achieve his purposes. The mis-
pronunciation of 'shibboleth' became the nemesis of
Ephraim.

Of deeper ethical and spiritual import are the words of
the Israelites with respect, firstly, to their calling upon God
for his help and, secondly, the dealings of the elders of
Gilead with Jephthah.

In the former case, the Lord challenged the sincerity of
their words (10:11–14). The Lord insisted upon words
that had real meaning. That is to say, he required that the
actions of Israel be consistent with their protestations of
faithfulness. The Lord had heard their words before, but
they still went back to their evil ways! Let them put away
their false gods now and then the Lord would see to it that
their prayer for deliverance was answered in the affirmative.
It must be a case of *ora et labora* — pray and work! Words
without actions constitute mere lip-service; let there be a
conjunction of word and deed in obedience to God's revealed
Word.

In the latter instance — the elders' dealings with Jephthah — the 'boomerang' effect of sinful words is clearly shown. The Lord made the elders of Gilead eat humble pie by obliging them to recall the very man that they had sinfully driven out years earlier. 'You may be sure that your sin will find you out,' said Moses to the children of Israel (Numbers 32:23). The rash and the harsh judgements that men make about their fellow men very soon return in the form of divine vindications of the truth. Perhaps the starkest example of this occurred on the *Dick Cavett Show*[4] a few years ago. A health-food enthusiast was on the show and he expatiated at great length on the benefits of good diet and predicted that he would, as a result of his own care in this matter, live on to a very advanced age. Another guest came in and as Cavett talked to him, he noticed the health-food man's head suddenly jerk forward. The man had died! The show was never aired. For anyone with eyes to see, the finger of God had pointed. The boast was invalidated within minutes of its utterance. God is not mocked. He will have every wicked, boastful, arrogant, idle, hurtful word eaten by the one who spoke it, either by true gospel repentance or by punishment in time and eternity.

The overarching point of application concerns Jephthah's vow. Many a Christian has made a commitment to God in a vow in connection with deliverance from some difficult situation. Men in the trenches have promised God that they would go into the gospel ministry if he spared them through the war. Pregnant women have promised a much-wanted daughter for missionary service, if indeed God gave a girl. How many men have had a life of frustration and fruitlessness in the ministry because they entered it, not out of any real conviction as to the gifts and the calling, but out of faithfulness to a rash vow? How many girls have had a wretched time trying to live with a mother who wanted them in the mission-field rather than married with three children in the next town?

So many vows turn to ashes, because, in the first place, God did not require them as a condition of his blessing and, in the second place, because they were in the nature

of bargaining with God. This does not mean that the Lord
has never blessed those who have taken rash vows. We are
inclined to believe that there was some 'oil of joy' even
for Jephthah's 'mourning'. God is a God of all grace and he
brings blessings not only in spite of our errors, but even in
and through them. We ought never to forget that every iota
of blessing in the lives of sinful human beings is free grace;
it is always undeserved and it always flows from the atonement which Christ made for the sins of his people on the
cross at Calvary. The believer who wrongly vowed his way
into the ministry, although his lack of gifts was to the contrary, will no doubt still have encouragements from the
Lord. The point still stands: voluntary vows are to be made
only when there is good evidence that their execution is
within our capabilities and with the clear understanding that
they are not bargaining chips in some deal with the Lord.

The question that remains to be answered is 'Does a rash
vow before the Lord have to be kept?' The answer to this
resolves on the question as to whether the vow is sinful or
not. A sinful vow is to be repented of (Leviticus 5:4,5).
A vow which is not sinful, but which turns out to involve
some loss — as in a business arrangement — is to be held to
faithfully (Psalm 15:4). Jephthah could have 'redeemed'
his daughter and thus relieved himself of the sorrow both
of them felt, but in the circumstances — not least of which
was her gentle acquiescence with his vow — he executed it
faithfully. Perhaps he felt that, as the leader in Israel, he
could hardly retain credibility and renege on a public vow
before God. We are not told every detail of his thinking.
He certainly did count the cost and went on to trust the
Lord.

This should not have the effect of inhibiting our public
commitments to the Lord. Rather it should stimulate us to
a careful faithfulness to Christ. The Lord Jesus Christ is
now revealed to us in all his grace and glory. The gospel
is a message of free and sovereign grace. The Lord has
promised to all who believe the gospel unto salvation that
his grace is sufficient for them (2 Cor. 12:9). Let our confession be in terms of simple obedience to his revealed will,

in dependence upon his sure promises and his sufficient grace.

> May the words of my mouth and the meditation
>   of my heart be pleasing in your sight,
>   O Lord, my Rock and my Redeemer.
> (Psalm 19:14).

Questions for further study:
1. Why did the Lord send the Ammonites and Philistines to oppress Israel? Had Israel progressed at all since the last period of backsliding? (10:6.)
2. Was the Lord satisfied with Israel's prayer for deliverance? If not, why not? (10:7—16.)
3. Who was Jephthah? (11:1—3.)
4. How did Jephthah come to lead Israel? (10:17,18; 11:4—11.) What did God teach the elders of Gilead in all this?
5. Why did war with Ammon become inveitable? Was Jephthah a poor negotiator? (11:12—28.) Consider the place of negotiation and war in the settling of international disputes.
6. Consider Jephthah's vow. What different views have been put forward to explain it? What does this teach us? (11:29—35.)
7. What was the attitude of his daughter? What does this teach us? (11:36—40.)
8. What caused civil war with the Ephraimites? How was that tribe punished? (12:1—7.)

References
1. John E. Hunter, *Judges and a Permissive Society*, Grand Rapids: 1975, Zondervan, pp. 92—93.
2. Another suggestion that has been made is that the text should be translated, '*or* I will sacrifice it as a burnt offering'. The idea is that Jephthah promised consecration to be the Lord's, if a human greeted him, *or* sacrifice by burnt offering, if a suitable animal presented itself. Keil and Delitzch (*Joshua and Judges,* p. 386) reject this interpretation.
3. G. C. M. Douglas, *The Book of Judges,* Edinburgh: T. and T. Clark, p. 65.
4. A television chat-show in the U.S.A.

11.
Dedicated from the womb

Please read Judges 13—16 and Hebrews 11

'A certain man of Zorah, named Manoah, from the clan of the Danites, had a wife who was sterile and remained childless. The angel of the Lord appeared to her and said, "You are sterile and childless, but you are going to conceive and have a son. Now see to it that you drink no wine or other fermented drink and that you do not eat anything unclean, because you will conceive and give birth to a son. No razor may be used on his head, because the boy is to be a Nazirite, set apart to God from birth, and he will begin the deliverance of Israel from the hands of the Philistines"'

(Judges 13:2—5).

With the advent of Samson, the period of the judges was drawing to a close. Samson judged Israel for twenty years (15:20) and, according to the consensus of Old Testament scholarship, these coincided with the second half of the Philistine forty-year oppression (13:1). This means that Samson probably ruled between the battle of Aphek, in which Israel was defeated and the ark of the covenant captured (1 Samuel 4:1—11), and the battle of Mizpah, in which Samuel crushed the Philistines and ended their oppression (1 Samuel 7:2—12). Samson, then, grew up at the time of Eli's ministry at Shiloh, began to lead Israel in the west as Jephthah was active in the east, that is, about the time of Eli's death, and continued until the prophet Samuel rose to the leadership of God's people. In terms of the overall sweep of the period of the judges, he began to lead Israel three hundred years after the passing away of Joshua's elders and he died some five years before the accession of Saul to the throne of Israel (1075 B.C.— 1055 B.C.).[1] One era was ending and another beginning, as the judges gave way to the kings of Israel. In our day there is constant debate between those who want less government and those who want more government. Government by judges, in Israel, was certainly 'less government', although it was very definitely theocratic in nature. The only permanent central government was the priesthood at Shiloh. The priesthood was to lead, guide and unify the semi-autonomous tribes of Israel. The judges were emergency leaders raised up for specific crises. This should have been sufficient, had Israel been faithful, but Israel was not faithful and the judges did not stop the rot. Israel was in a state of anarchy in Samson's day and the Lord then brought in the theocratic monarchy. More government was necessary because of the sin of the people, but in the inscrutable wisdom of God, it was designed to point to the ultimate truth that there was to be only one King for the people of God — the Son of David, the promised Messiah, the Lord Jesus Christ, Zion's King and Head. In the end the political system is beside the point; the question is 'Will the Lord be our King?'

Set apart to God

The history of Samson, as recorded in Judges 13—16, is in two parts. The first is composed of Judges 13—15 and records his birth and his rise to leadership, while the second, Judges 16, makes it evident that most of the twenty years of Samson's judgeship lies between chapters 15 and 16. It seems reasonable to assume that during that long period Samson served the Lord faithfully and, if he did not exactly remove the Philistines, he must have minimized the effects of their aggression. It is vital for us to grasp this concept of Samson's ministry, because too often he is thought of only in terms of the often questionable' behaviour recorded in

Judges 14–16. These chapters, however, record a very small proportion of his life — namely the summer before he became judge and the last year of his life. That Samson served God faithfully is a perspective that must not be obscured even by his manifest sins, for without this perspective — as will be shown later — the meaning of Samson's life will be seriously misunderstood (cf. Hebrews 11:32). In this study we shall focus upon the rise of this man of God to the judgeship, leaving his decline and fall for a separate chapter.

An entire chapter is devoted to the nativity of Samson (13:1–25). The Angel of the Lord, the second person of the Trinity, appeared to the wife of a Danite, named Manoah. He told her that, although she was sterile and childless, she would conceive and bear a son and that son would be consecrated to the Lord as a deliverer for his people (13:2–4). She believed him, in spite of not having recognized him as God, and immediately told her husband, Manoah. He believed her but, like Gideon before him, he wanted confirmation. The Angel of the Lord did subsequently appear to them and he confirmed his earlier word, first by declaration and then by consuming Manoah's sacrifice with fire and ascending in the flames (13:13,14,19,20). In due time the boy was born and called Samson. 'He grew and the Lord blessed him, and the Spirit of the Lord began to stir him . . .' (13:24,25).

There are, in this account of Samson's origins, two principal features which together form the basic perspective necessary to any understanding of his significance in the history of God's plan of redemption.

The first is that his birth was announced by the Angel of the Lord and confirmed by the acceptance of a sacrifice. Samson is thus placed in the company of Isaac — the only other person in Scripture whose birth was announced in a similar fashion (Genesis 18:9–15). Samson, then, was raised up for a major role in God's purpose of redemption for his people.

The second significant point is that Samson was dedicated from the womb to a perpetual Nazirite vow. Edersheim asserts — correctly, I believe — that 'The meaning of Samson's history is that he was a Nazirite.'[2] The 'Nazirite vow' was provided for in the law of God, in Numbers 6. It was a means of spiritual consecration distinct from that of the priests and it involved, as the badges of that consecration, three specific observances. There was to be abstinence from wine and, indeed, grapes themselves; there was to be no cutting of the hair; and no coming into the presence of dead bodies, i.e. entering a house of mourning.[3] In modern terms, Nazirites were long-haired total abstainers, who could not visit funeral parlours! Of course, they were far more than these external signs. These were badges of consecration — long hair, for instance, signified subjection to the Lord[4] — and Nazirites were to be noted for practical godliness. Nazirite vows were voluntary and for a specified duration, but Samson's consecration was decreed by God and was for life. This further indicated the nature of his role. He was called to be a deliverer and, as such, an example of devotion to the Lord for his people.

God's 'loner'

The fourteenth and fifteenth chapters of Judges outline the series of events which propelled Samson into the position for which he had been born. He must have been in early adulthood around the time of Israel's loss of the ark of the covenant at Aphek (1 Samuel 4). The Philistine hegemony was now uncontested and so the time was ripe for the deliverer to arise. Samson, under the influence of the Spirit of God, sought an occasion to confront the Philistines (14:4) and since he had a notion for a Philistine girl in Timnah, he took steps to win her for his wife — perhaps hoping that in some way his contact with Philistines would give opportunity to redress the Israelite grievances. He may well, however, have had no such ideas and may have simply been led, in the providence of God, into a situation where God himself would use him to work out his as yet secret purpose. In any event, there was no prohibition in the law

against marriage to Philistines, although the claims of true
godliness would suggest that Manoah's advice to Samson
not to marry outside Israel was sound.

Samson was determined, however, and went to Timnah
to make the arrangements. On the way, he was attacked
by a young lion but, with the enabling power of the Spirit
of God, he tore it apart with his bare hands (14:1—7).

Some time later, on the way down to Timnah for the
wedding, he passed the lion's carcass — it must have been
little more than bones by this time — and, finding a swarm
of bees and their honeycombs in it, he took some honey
and ate it. This suggested a riddle to him which he proposed
to his thirty Philistine groomsmen as the focus of a wager:

> Out of the eater, something to eat;
> out of the strong, something sweet.

If they solved it Samson would give each of them a new
change of clothing. If they could not solve it then they
would give Samson thirty changes of clothing (14:8—14).
The Philistine lads were baffled and angry. So they contrived
to have Samson's bride find the solution. They told her
that if she didn't find it and tell them, then they would
burn her and her father in their own house. Rather than
resist them and trust her new husband, she did as they said.
Samson lost his wager, and now he was angry, because he
realized he had been tricked. This spurred Samson to action
against the Philistines. Under the influence of the Spirit of
God, Samson went to Ashkelon, killed thirty men, took
their clothes and gave them to the groomsmen. He then
left in anger and his bride was given by her father to one
of the thirty (14:15—20). Why Samson killed thirty men
in Ashkelon rather than the men at Timnah is not revealed
to us. Suffice it to say that with this action Samson set
his course for the rest of his life.

Some time later, at the wheat harvest, Samson decided
to go back to Timnah to claim his wife. When he was
rebuffed by her father, he reacted by destroying the Philistines' crops. This he did by the not inconsiderable feat of

capturing three hundred foxes and releasing them, in pairs, tied tail to tail with a torch tied to each pair, to run wild through the fields (15:1–5).

From this point on the conflict escalated very rapidly. Samson's wife and father-in-law were burnt to death by the Philistines, who blamed them, quite unjustly, for their troubles (15:6). In a reprisal raid Samson killed many of them (15:7,8). The Philistines then sent strong forces into Israel to look for Samson. This persuaded the men of Judah to deliver Samson into their hands. Samson, for his part, was very enthusiastic about any opportunity to close with the enemy and consented to be handed over. Again the Spirit of the Lord endowed this already strong man with greater might and he killed 1,000 Philistines with the jawbone of a donkey (15:9–17).

All this the Lord used to establish Samson as the leader of Israel. Samson thereafter was the champion of God's people and the scourge of his enemies. Samson recognized that this was the work of God when he declared, 'You have given your servant this great victory.' Then the Lord sealed the truth of this to him by miraculously providing water to slake his thirst after the battle (15:18–20).

Samson did not lead any armies. He did not conquer the Philistines, but for twenty years he was a restraint upon them, for by his exploits and prestige he occupied their attentions and must therefore have relieved the pressure upon Israel. Napoleon once remarked that the Duke of Wellington's *name* was worth 10,000 men. How much greater in the minds of the Philistines the name of Samson must have been! He was truly the scourge of the Philistine nation. In this way Samson led Israel faithfully for twenty years. He was God's 'loner' for the sake of God's people.

The meaning of Samson for today

There are three basic approaches to the question of Samson's meaning for the church in our own age.

One is to view him as a man who 'had everything' but

ended up a backslidden failure.[5] It is true that the recorded
incidents in Judges 14—16 show us a man who was seriously
flawed and who, towards the end of his life, was over-
whelmed by his own lust. To focus on his sins — as one must
do to see him principally as a failure — is not to see the wood
for the trees. It is to miss the point of Hebrews 11:32 and to
fail to reckon with the actual thrust of the text of Judges.
Whatever *we* may disapprove of in Samson's rise to judgeship, *the Lord* did approve and we have no reason to believe
that Samson was unfaithful during his long ministry as judge,
until the backsliding towards the end. More will be said in
the next chapter on his failings, but suffice it to say at this
point that the evidence points to faithfulness in spite of
failings and Hebrews 11:32 is the final proof of this. When
it comes to making application, the failure perspective
inevitably produces a series of moralistic lessons mostly
orientated to avoiding Samson's sins. He ran after heathen
women; he gambled and kept bad company; he was
impetuous and had a vengeful spirit; he was self-centred;
and we should take care not to be like him in these things.
Far be it from anyone to minimize Samson's faults. The
sins of the saints are as much of an example for us not to
follow as their godliness is for us to imitate. In understanding the meaning of Samson, however, it is secondary to the
fundamental perspective that he was God's man for the
hour. He has a greater significance for God's people in every
age than as a mere provider of a few moral lessons and a
generally bad example. He was one of those whom God
'commended for their faith' (Hebrews 11:39). This positive
perspective is the key to the proper application of Samson's
life and ministry to the church in all ages. Failure is not the
dominant theme.

The second approach tends to go in the opposite direction
and view Samson, not as basically a failure, but as a type,
or foreshadowing, of Christ. Again the focus is on the details
of his life — not on his sins but on those aspects which
supposedly prefigure elements in the life and ministry of
the Lord Jesus Christ. There is his miraculous birth; his
Nazirite vow; his battling with the 'roaring lion'; his

permitting himself to be bound and delivered by his own people into the hands of the enemy as the price of their safety; his role as deliverer of Israel and his self-sacrifice in Dagon's Temple. All these are seen as establishing Samson as a foreshadowing — a living prophetic picture — of Christ. Of course, to do so involves, at best, special pleading and, at worst, fanciful spiritualization of the text. Every point cannot be argued, but let it be asked by what canons of sound exegesis does Samson's encounter with the lion prefigure Christ's temptations in the wilderness? Is there really a prefiguring of the virgin birth of Christ in Samson's birth to a hitherto childless woman who was certainly not a virgin? It is one thing to understand Samson, in his capacity as a God-appointed judge, as a kind of symbol of the hope of a Saviour yet to be revealed to Israel — more of this in a moment — but it is something else again to turn the slightest details of his life into prophecies about the Lord Jesus Christ. Samson's life is not an allegory about Jesus — as Bunyan's *Pilgrim's Progress* is an allegory about the Christian life — but it is a milestone in the history of redemption which gives a hint of better things to come. Can the cross really be seen in Samson's destruction of the Temple of Dagon? Surely not! Let us not substitute airy spiritualization for solid exposition of the text of Scripture. To do so would be to render Samson more a figure of speech than a figure of history.

How then are we to understand Samson? When we view his life in the context of the whole period of the judges, we are led to the conclusion that he is almost a personification of Israel during that time. It is not that he is merely a symbol of Israel's failure, but rather that he symbolizes the hope of a Saviour yet to be revealed in and through Israel. Samson is, in a sense, Israel of the judges. Israel was to be a Nazirite people — not in the literal sense that everyone should take a Nazirite vow, but in the sense that that which the Nazirite vow stood for, holiness unto God, should be the spiritual state of the people as a whole. Samson's strength was in his Nazirite faithfulness and his weakness came as he departed from his vow and gave himself to sinful

passions. The strength was not, of course, in abstinence
from the fruit of the grape and haircuts. Christ himself
was not a Nazirite. These were only the external badges
of inward spiritual devotion. Israel, like Samson, was
brought low when she committed spiritual adultery. The
Lord, none the less, had a purpose of grace and salvation
for them. Samson and Israel belonged to God and they stand,
in the end, as trophies of grace. Samson does not foreshadow
Christ, but he points to the need for Christ and to the
promise of deliverance which only can be truly realized in
his finished work of atonement for sin. In Samson, God is
triumphant over sin, certainly in the deliverances of twenty
years of judgeships, but most pointedly in the ruins of
Dagon's Temple. If therefore we can identify with Samson
in terms of our own battles with sin in our lives, then all
the more must we rejoice with him in the victories of the
Lord over his enemies.

The great practical question for us is 'Are we trusting in
the Saviour in whom Samson trusted from "afar off" '? Are
we seeking the constant enabling power of the Holy Spirit
whose power gave Samson his amazing victories? Are we
seeking to be approved of the same God, whose final comment upon Samson is that he was commended for his faith?
(Hebrews 11.) Samson's awareness of the light of the gospel
was limited; to us the light is abundantly available through
the Lord Jesus Christ. Let us deny ourselves, take up the
cross and follow him, even the blessed Son of God, Christ
Jesus! (Mark 8:34.)

Questions for further study:
1. Review in broad outline the period of the judges and
   fix the position of Samson in relation to the Philistine
   oppression, Jephthah, Eli and Samuel (Judges 10:7;
   13:1; 15:20; 1 Samuel 7:2—12.)
2. Compare the account of the appearance of the Angel of
   the Lord to Samson's parents with that of his meeting
   with Gideon (Judges 6:11—23; 13:2—21). What are the
   similarities? What does it all mean? (Cf. also Genesis
   18:9—15.)

3. Consider the Nazirite vow (Numbers 6:1−8). What did it signify? Why was Samson to be a Nazirite?
4. How did the Spirit of God deal with Samson? Is there a difference between this and the way the Holy Spirit deals with believers in the New Testament?
5. How did Samson come to the position of judge over Israel? Does Judges 14:4 indicate the Lord's approval of everything Samson did?
6. What was Israel's sin against Samson? (15:12.) What does Judges 15:14−20 tell us of the nature of salvation?
7. What was different about Samson's judgeship when compared with the other judges? In the light of this consider the meaning of Samson for the church in both the Old and New Testaments.
8. How is Samson an example for us? (Hebrews 11:32− 12:12.)

References
1. The chronology of this period is very difficult to unravel. The most satisfactory account I have discovered is in Leon Wood, *The Distressing Days of the Judges*, pp. 10−17. There is a chronological chart on pp. 409−411.
2. Alfred Edersheim, *Bible History: Old Testament*, Wilmington: Associated Publishers and Authors, p. 232.
3. For a helpful exposition of the Nazirite vow see Patrick Fairbairn, *The Typology of Scripture*, II, 367−72.
4. Cf. 1 Corinthians 11:2−16 where the same idea is applied in the relation of the woman to the authority of the man.
5. e.g. John Hunter, *Judges and a Permissive Society*, Grand Rapids: Zondervan, 1975.

12.
Defeat into victory

Please read Judges 16

'Then Samson prayed to the Lord, "O Sovereign Lord, remember me. O God, please strengthen me just once more, and let me with one blow get revenge on the Philistines for my two eyes"' (Judges 16:28).

There is, as G. C. M. Douglas wrote a century ago, 'a tragic grandeur in the decline and fall of the Hebrew republic, when the last of the ordinary judges gave himself up to die for the redemption of his country'.[1] This 'ordinary judge' was extraordinarily larger than life. So much so, perhaps, that there is a tendency to treat him as a mythical figure — a kind of biblical 'Superman', whose 'unreal' exploits somehow or other provide us with a real impetus to serve God. This has to be resisted. This is sober history, not mythology, and our perspective must be that of Hebrews 11 — Samson as a man 'commended for his faith', and not that of the Hollywood 'biblical epic' movie. Samson was raised up by God to punish the oppressors and to deliver the oppressed people of God. He was therefore strengthened by the Lord so that he could do by himself what ordinarily would have required the whole nation.

Walking on hot coals

The downfall of Samson can be summed up in words written in the Proverbs, warning against unhallowed sexual desires:

Do not lust in your heart after her beauty
    or let her captivate you with her eyes,
for the prostitute reduces you to a loaf of bread,
    and the adulteress preys upon your very life.
Can a man scoop fire into his lap
    without his clothes being burned?
Can a man walk on hot coals
    without his feet being scorched?

(Proverbs 6:25–28)

If there was an indication in Samson's earlier life of an
intensely passionate nature – in particular, his desire to
marry the Philistine girl from Timnah – it now, in his latter
days, assumed the proportions of an enslavement to a
besetting sin. The first three verses of Judges 16 are best
understood as an indication of this problem in his life. This
provides the context in which his seduction and betrayal
by Delilah can be seen as the inevitable catastrophic end of
a way of life devoted to the mere satisfaction of lust. Samson
went to Gaza, some believe in order to spy out the Philistines
or provoke another confrontation. Whatever he had his eye
on, it did not stay there for long. Like Job he should have
'made a covenant with [his] eyes not to look lustfully at a
girl' (Job 31:1), but he saw a prostitute and, like the fellow
in the camera advertisement on TV, who swings the camera
away from the tennis action to the sexy-looking girl coming
on to the court, Samson turned his attention to her . . . and
then went to spend the night with her (16:1). The Philistines
observed this and planned to wait through the night and kill
him at dawn when he would try to slip out of the city
(16:2). Samson, contrary to their expectations, did not stay
all night, but left at midnight and not only did he escape
unharmed, he smashed the gate and carried it away, posts
and all, to deposit it on a hilltop miles away (16:3). It has
been suggested that Samson terminated his dalliance with
the prostitute at midnight, because he realized that he had
been side-tracked into sin, when he should have been doing
the Lord's work of chastising these Philistines. As to guilt
and repentance, we are told nothing directly. Many a

Christian indulging in a besetting sin 'comes to himself', by God's grace, as did the prodigal son (Luke 15:17) and flees that place where he is steeping himself in his sin. 'O God,' he cries, 'why am I here in this harlot's bed, when I know the commandments of the Lord and love the Saviour who bought me with his own blood?' Whether this was true of Samson, or not, remains an open question. What is certain is that the Lord was with him still and caused him to humiliate the Philistines in an amazing way. Samson's strength — the blessing of the Lord — was with him . . . but the writing was on the wall, for his sins were beginning to find him out (Daniel 5; Numbers 32:23).

A little later Samson took up with a Philistine woman called Delilah. Her name has become a byword for seduction. He became infatuated with her and apparently was a regular visitor at her house. There is no talk of marriage. There is no apparent shame either, which, by the way, is a comment on the supposed modernity of twentieth-century 'moral freedom' (a euphemism for old-fashioned immoral bondage!). Samson, like the hero in the film *Twelve Chairs*, was 'very much in lust' with his girl . . . and the Philistines knew it. They offered Delilah a tidy sum in return for the key to overpowering Samson, i.e. 'the secret of his great strength' (16:4,5). She agreed and began to work on him. Samson at first seemed to treat it as a huge joke and he would spin a yarn about how he could be subdued. First it was 'seven thongs'; then it was 'new ropes'; and on another occasion he told her that the seven braids of his hair would have to be woven into 'the fabric on the loom'. Three times she tested what he had said, tying him up in the prescribed manner while he was asleep and then awakening him with the shout: 'Samson, the Philistines are upon you!' Each time, he broke free with ease and the Philistines hiding in the next room had to sneak away (16:6—14).

It had been an amusing diversion to Samson, thus far — just the sort of silly game lovers tend to play, you might say. The joke was over, however, and that is evident in Delilah's new ploy: 'How can you say, "I love you," when

you won't confide in me?' This was the first direct challenge
of Samson's allegiance to the living God. It was the first
direct test of the strength of the web of seduction that
Delilah had woven around Samson's heart. Now Israel's
judge would discover what the writer of the Proverbs was
to inscripturate years later: 'The mouth of an adulteress
is a deep pit; he who is under the Lord's wrath will fall into
it' (Proverbs 22:14).

Samson told Delilah the secret of his strength. He had
been a Nazirite from birth and his hair had never been cut.
'If my head were shaved, my strength would leave me, and
I would become as weak as any other man' (16:17). Delilah
made arrangements, as before, to have the Philistines standing by. She had his long hair cut while he was asleep and
again cried out, 'Samson, the Philistines are upon you!'
Samson awoke and immediately thought that he could deal
with any threat as he had in times past. 'But he did not
know that the Lord had left him.' He was captured, his
eyes were gouged out — that remained a standard method
of rendering great men harmless in parts of the East even
into the modern era[2] — and he was put to hard work as a
prisoner in Gaza, grinding corn for his enemies (16:18–21).

The wages of sin

Hair grows and, for the Nazirite whose head has been shaven,
this signifies the renewal of the vow. It is not that there was
anything magical or virtuous about the hair itself. When
Samson lost his hair, it was not that in itself which drained
his strength. It was rather the fact — which he refused to
recognize at the time — that the Lord had left him. Samson
was unfaithful. That his hair was cut was merely symbolic
of the departure of the Lord from him. As it grew and as
he languished under that supreme symbol of his failure, the
Philistine yoke, there was a reviving of true faith in his heart
and he no doubt began to pray for the return of the Lord's
favour.

That moment came at the feast of thanksgiving to Dagon,

the fish-god. The flower of Philistia gathered for the festivities and crowded into the temple where this huge idol, which two decades earlier had toppled over before the captured ark of the covenant (1 Samuel 5:4), now stood defiantly in opposition to the living God. Placed next to the pillars that held up the roof of the temple, Samson cried to God for strength that he might wreak his vengeance upon the Philistines. 'Let me die with the Philistines!' he cried as he moved the pillars and with a roar the whole structure collapsed and thousands perished (16:23–30).

So ends the period of the judges. Samson's relatives retrieved his body from the rubble — apparently without interference from a presumably cowed and terrified Philistine populace — and the last judge was laid to rest in the tomb of his father (16:31).

'The wages of sin,' as Paul teaches in Romans 6:23, 'is death.' This is true for both physical and spiritual (eternal) death. Samson suffered physical death because he was a sinner. We will all experience physical death — unless we are alive at the Lord's return (1 Thessalonians 4:17) — because we too are sinners (Romans 5:12). But salvation means that spiritual death is conquered, and that, at the resurrection, physical death too is reversed. Death is swallowed up in victory! (1 Corinthians 15:54.) And that victory affects the present life of the believer, even in the face of the shortness of his life. Death, the last enemy, can be faced triumphantly in God's strength (1 Corinthians 15:55–58.) Samson's death is, you see, a triumph of grace over sin and of that Hebrews 11:32 is the proof. For the Philistines, it is the summons to a lost eternity. Blessing and curse are in the same action. God's love for one and his wrath for many are memorialized in the fall of Dagon's Temple.

The great question

The problem that faces all who look into the life of Samson is how to reconcile his terrible decline and fall with his equally evident approval by God. 'How could Samson be a true believer?' is the great question.

In the last chapter we sought to show that Samson was neither a backslidden failure, providing only an example for us *not* to follow, nor a 'type' of Christ in which the details of his life — from his birth to his death with outstretched arms — are spiritualized into prophetic pictures of the person and work of the Messiah. We saw him, rather, as a symbol of Israel of the judges, to be sure, showing forth the sinfulness of God's people in that time, but above all symbolizing the hope of a greater Saviour yet to be revealed.

Yes, Samson was in many ways a wayward character. In his desire to exact revenge at every turn he appeared even at the end to be tainted still with that vindictive spirit which showed up early in his life. So even when he called upon the Lord, he focused his mind upon himself: 'Let *me* with one blow get revenge on the Philistines for *my* two eyes' (16:28). There can be no doubt that he had repented of his former sin with Delilah and was now restored to a happy relationship with the Lord, but the old flaw still remained. His licentiousness was a more dramatic fault. It was, as Charles Simeon put it, 'his great failing . . . Verily the fetters of brass did not form a stronger bond for his feet, than ungoverned passions make for the souls of men. Even reason and common sense often appear to fail the persons who are under their influence; insomuch that, with temporal and eternal ruin before their eyes, they rush on, till they bring upon themselves the miseries which they would not shun.'[3]

How then are we to assess Samson, the man of God? There are perhaps four significant points which help to place his character in proper perspective and indicate also how God's people can be greatly edified by the consideration of his life.

In the first place, it must be remembered that Samson lived in a time when God was not yet prepared to reveal himself with all the fulness of the gospel now revealed to us in Christ through the pages of a completed Scripture. This is not to lead us to minimize his shortcomings, but it is to help us understand the way in which truth has been revealed progressively down the centuries of God's dealing with men. In the light of David's sin with Bathsheba and the murder of Uriah and the licentiousness of Solomon in his latter days, we will be less censorious of Samson, while at the same time we realize how wonderful the patience of the Lord really is. The Christian of the New Testament era has more light than Samson ever did, but, truth to tell, he still has the same old darkness clinging to him. If anything, we have less excuse, because we are given far more.

In the second place, no real Christian can fail to be touched by a sense of fellowship with Samson in his experience with the power of sin within his own members. The offended tone of some Christian writing on Samson suggests the possibility of a certain lack of self-knowledge in the writers. When a sinner knows what it really is to be a sinner — one who offends God's perfect holiness — then he is moved to compassion rather than indignant self-righteousness. Christ did not sin, but was tempted in all points as we are, and therefore was all the more moved by our plight.

In the third place, the Lord shows us, in the downfall of Samson, the folly of trusting in gifts as if they had been self-produced and belonged to us for ever, whatever our practical relationship to the Lord. The Lord often lets us fall just to remind us that there is no goodness or strength or gifts and graces outside of a saving relationship to him. Without the exercise of a living faith, all is vanity. Samson discovered this to his cost and his very apotheosis in the ruins of the temple is a testimony to this truth. Spiritual gifts are just that — gifts of the Spirit. We must watch our hearts, otherwise the best of gifts will fail.

Fourthly, we ought to remember that the Lord raised up Samson to personify Israel of the judges, in all its wavering devotion and terrible backsliding. That period is buried with Samson, but it must not be forgotten that simultaneously in the life of Israel a new era of grace and favour was dawning in the ministry of another lifelong Nazirite, the prophet Samuel. Samson, in a way, points to Samuel as John the Baptizer points to Christ. As the one must decrease, the other must increase. God's people saw this new reformation happening before their eyes — the crash of Dagon's Temple would not be seen as the *Last Post* for an age gone by as much as *Reveille* for an era of spiritual revival. Thus at Mizpah Samuel gathered the repentant people of God in calling for his aid against the Philistines. The Lord heard and showed his love for Israel in breaking the power of their enemies (1 Samuel 7).

So it is for God's people in every age. God is not withholding spiritual blessing for which we are asking. 'Test me in this . . . and see if I will not throw open the floodgates of heaven and pour out so much blessing that you will not have room enough for it' (Malachi 3:10). Samson brings us to the cross, for in the death of Christ as the sin-bearer for all who believe in him is the fountain opened for all uncleanness. In Christ, says Paul, 'are hidden all the treasures of wisdom and knowledge' (Col. 2:3).

Questions for further study:
1. What led to Samson's fall? Consider the concept of Numbers 32:23 and find examples from Scripture (e.g. 2 Samuel 12:1–7.)
2. Consider Proverbs 6:25–28; 22:14 and Job 31:1 in relation to our lives today. Why is so much television (programming and commercials) so destructive? What should be done about it?
3. Consider Delilah's seduction of Samson. What did she do to break down his resistance? What is the significance of Judges 16:15?
4. Was Samson's strength in the hair itself? (16:20.) Review the nature of the Nazirite vow. What did the growth of his hair while in captivity signify?
5. Did Samson repent of his sins? Was his death suicide (clue: was he just trying to kill himself?) or was it self-sacrifice? How did God's blessing of his people and his wrath against the wicked manifest themselves in the festivities at Gaza?
6. Was Samson a true believer? What factors point to an affirmative answer to this question?

7. What was happening in Israel at the same time as Samson came to his end in Gaza? (1 Samuel 7:2—13.)
8. What does it mean for the church to be 'always reforming' (*semper reformanda*)? Does your church need reformation?

References
1. George C. M. Douglas, D.D., *The Book of Judges*, p. 80. Douglas was the Principal of the Free Church College, Glasgow in the nineteenth century and an eminent Old Testament scholar.
2. Until the nineteenth century the deposed Kings of Afghanistan could expect to be blinded. They were rarely killed. Alive, but blind, they remained as a constant reminder of the power of those who had deposed them.
3. C. Simeon, *Expository Outlines on the Whole Bible*, Vol. 3, p. 75.

13.
The stranger from Moab

Please read Ruth 1

'Where you go I will go, and where you stay I will stay.
Your people will be my people and your God my God.
Where you die I will die, and there I will be buried.
May the Lord deal with me, be it ever so severely, if
anything but death separates you and me'

(Ruth 1:16,17).

The book of Ruth has been called 'a summer's morning
after a night of wild tempest'.[1] So sweet does it seem in
contrast to the blood-curdling narratives which precede
and follow it that the tendency is not to think of it as history
at all, but as some kind of poetic interlude — a timeless
witness to eternal verities, a legend conveying moral
instruction rather than a real piece of Israel's history. The
fact is, of course, that Ruth is an account of social and
religious life in Bethlehem during the period of the judges.
As such it serves to record two vital facts that bear upon
the whole subsequent life and progress of God's people
right down to our own day and so gives us a perspective
on the time of the judges which is not to be found in the
book of Judges itself.

It reminds us, in the first instance, that even in the darkest
of times the work of the Lord goes on in the faithfulness
of a godly remnant. In Bethlehem, as no doubt in many
otherwise insignificant corners of Israel, there was a
community marked by piety. Life was quiet and peaceful,
for the most part, and the grace of God was manifestly
evident in the life of the people. We are reminded of the

beautiful words of Scotland's national poet, Robert Burns, when he recalled the simple godliness of his rural upbringing in his poem, *The Cotter's Saturday Night.* Having described the family worship in the cottager's home, he tells about the prayers of the parents for their children:

> Then homeward all take off their several way;
>   The youngling cottagers retire to rest;
> The parent-pair their secret homage pay,
>   and proffer up to Heaven the warm request
> That he who stills the raven's clam'rous nest
> And decks the lily fair in flowery pride,
>   Would, in the way his wisdom sees the best,
> For them and for their little ones provide;
>   But, chiefly, in their hearts with Grace Divine preside.

The Lord continues his work of redemption, whatever the circumstances may be, and continues to add to the church such as he purposes to save. Thus Ruth, the foreigner from Moab, was converted to the Lord and became one of his people.

A second point of significance, which will be examined in the next chapter, is the fact that Ruth was to become the mother of David's grandfather, Obed, and therefore was a direct ancestress of the Lord Jesus Christ. Ruth, like Esther in a later generation, is not remembered in the Scriptures merely because she is a fine example of godly womanhood, but because she is a vital figure in the history of God's work of redemption. Esther is the one person who was used by God to save his whole people from destruction — an event which would have ended the work of redemption. Ruth is a significant link in the chain of descent that leads to a Bethlehem stable.

Ruth and Naomi

The events recorded in the book of Ruth are generally believed to have taken place during the judgeship of Gideon, perhaps some eighty years before the death of Samson.[2] There was at that time a famine in Bethlehem, which is ironic when one remembers that Bethlehem means, literally, 'house of bread'. A man named Elimelech, his wife Naomi and their two sons, Mahlon and Kilion, left that village, and Israel itself, and emigrated to Moab, beyond the Jordan. What a comment upon the state of Israel that God's people should be hungry and Moab be experiencing plenty! (Leviticus 26:19,20.) It is the believer's duty to provide for his family (1 Timothy 5:8) and no doubt this was Elimelech's motive in moving, but it must be said that it is difficult to see it as a move made in faithfulness to God's promises. Elimelech ought not to have fled to a foreign land. To do so was to admit a lack of trust that the Lord would provide for them in the land of promise. It can only be understood as the triumph of pragmatism over faith. It is, also, a story oft repeated in the lives of Christians today – Elimelech ought to have stayed, in the spirit of the Salvation Army officer in Shanghai in 1949, who said in his last cable before the Communists arrived: 'I'm sitting in the premises and standing on the Promises!' Subsequent events tend to confirm this judgement. First, Elimelech died (1:3) and then, some years later, his two sons also died (1:5). This left Naomi and her two daughters-in-law, Orpah and Ruth – the Moabite girls that the two boys had married.[3] Within ten years of leaving Bethlehem, Naomi was bereft of her husband and sons and with her Moabite daughters-in-law had to face the world alone (1:1–5).

In the meantime, conditions had improved in Judah and so Naomi decided to return home. She urged the girls to stay in Moab and prayed for God's blessing for them, not least in the finding of husbands. They demurred, but Naomi insisted, reminding them that she was too old to provide sons for them to marry (this under the levirate principle of Deuteronomy 25:5–10).[4] Naomi was gripped by a deep sorrow at the loss of her posterity, for she confessed, 'It is more bitter for me than for you, because the Lord's hand has gone out against me!' In other words: 'Stay in Moab. There you can find husbands. There you can have the posterity that I shall never have.' Oh, how agonizing it must have been for Naomi to look back on that day ten years before when she and her husband and sons had turned their backs on God's promises! (1:6–13.) God is gracious and for those that love him it really is true that every cloud has a silver lining! Orpah turned back, but Ruth refused to leave her. '"Look," said Naomi, "your sister-in-law is going back to her people and her gods. Go back with her"' (1:14,15).

Ruth, however, was no longer committed to 'her people and her gods' and, in one of the most beautiful confessions of living faith ever made, she declared her resolve to go with Naomi back to Bethlehem. 'There is such ardour and earnestness about [Ruth's words]', said Alfred Edersheim, 'as to lift them far above the sphere of mere natural affection or sense of duty. They intimate the deliberate choice of a heart which belongs in the first place to Jehovah, the God of Israel, and which has learned to count all things but loss for the excellency of this knowledge.'[5] The beauty of her words is unsurpassed in the rendering of the Authorized Version of 1611: 'And Ruth said, Intreat me not to leave thee, or to return from following after thee: for whither thou goest, I will go; and where thou lodgest, I will lodge: thy people shall be my people, and thy God my God: where thou diest, will I die, and there will I be buried: the Lord do so to me, and more also, if ought but death part thee and me' (1:16,17.) With this the matter was settled. The stranger from Moab was now openly and irrevocably committed to the Lord and to his people. She who was not a Jew outwardly, after the flesh, had become, by grace through faith, a Jew inwardly and had cast her lot with God's people (cf. Romans 2:28,29).

Naomi and Ruth must have caused quite a stir when they trudged into Bethlehem at the harvest time that year. Doubtless the grief of ten years of difficulty and tragic bereavement showed in Naomi's face and brought forth the exclamation of the women: 'Can this be Naomi?' 'Naomi' means 'gracious', but Naomi asked that they call her 'Mara', which means 'bitter' — not because she was bitter in her heart, but because her experience had been a bitter one. 'I went away full, but the Lord has brought me back empty . . . The Lord has afflicted me; the Almighty has brought misfortune upon me' (1:20,21). 'Every rod has a voice, the voice of witness,' said one of the old writers. 'No discipline seems pleasant at the time, but painful,' wrote the writer of the Epistle to the Hebrews. 'Later on, however, it produces a harvest of righteousness and peace for those who have been trained by it' (Hebrews 12:11). More than barley would be harvested for Naomi and Ruth in days to come as Ruth, 'amidst the alien corn', became the channel of great blessing to them both and to God's people in every age.

True conversion

The recurrent tendency in the application of the message of the book of Ruth has been to clothe it in an aura of romance and to focus primarily upon the relationship between Ruth and Naomi. As we seek to understand this message, we need to be clear about two things in particular.

The first is that, although Ruth's confession in 1:16,17 is the central theme of the chapter, it is not the central meaning of the whole book. To many this is probably a new and rather shocking thought, because there is no question that the sweetest words in this book, which abounds with sweet words, are those which Ruth spoke to Naomi. Wonderful words they are, and they are rich with application to our own hearts and lives, as will shortly be made clear, but they are only preparatory to deeper revelation of the gospel that follows in the later chapters, culminating in the astounding fact that Ruth was to be a direct ancestor of David and of our Lord himself. We must look through Ruth's sublime confession of love for her mother-in-law to its centre, to God, the Lord, to the one who was to come, the Lord Jesus Christ. We will see more of this in our next study.

Secondly, when this basic Christ-centred perspective is grasped, we will begin to see how Ruth's confession should

and should not be understood. It is often applied to
'romantic' love, when in fact there is no romantic love in
the text. As Edersheim put it, 'Only the sternest prose of
poverty is before her.' Naomi had been completely candid
about her prospects if she should come with her and Ruth's
choice is intelligible only in terms of her conversion to the
Lord and consequent faith-commitment to his people.
Ruth's confession is a confession of faith and of what we
call Christian love (Gk., *agape*). There is, of course, a deep
personal commitment of Ruth to her mother-in-law. The
root of this is a shared saving faith in the living God and
it is upon this faith that the passage principally focuses.

What is the point? It is to teach us, albeit in terms of
the limited revelation of the Old Testament, about the
gospel and specifically about the meaning of true conversion
to the Lord. There are five points that should be noticed.

First and foremost is *commitment to the living God, who
reveals himself in the Bible.* 'Your God' will be 'my God'.
Ruth had been brought up to believe in Chemosh, the god
of the Moabites, but now she had chosen to follow the God
of Israel. She sealed this with the words: 'The Lord do so
to me and more also' (1:17 AV), using the covenant name
of God, Jehovah, and thus confessing her new relationship
to him. She had a personal relationship with God. She
called him '*my* God' (1:16) not with the casual blasphemy
of so much modern conversation, but reverently out of a
renewed heart. The first part of true conversion is just this —
to know God out of a changed heart. In New Testament
terms we know God only through his Son as the explicitly
revealed object of our faith. Ruth believed in the Saviour
'afar off', like all the Old Testament saints. We are called
to believe on the Lord Jesus Christ because he has come
and finished his atoning work for the salvation of sinners.
And the truly converted person can look any man in the eye
and say, 'I know whom I have believed, and am convinced
that he is able to guard what I have entrusted to him'
(2 Timothy 1:12).

A second facet of Ruth's commitment is *commitment
to the Lord's people.* 'Your people will be my people.'

This necessarily flows from a real commitment to the Lord. Immediately after his conversion on the Damascus road, the apostle Paul spent several days with the very people he had been intending to persecute. The effect of Pentecost was to create a church — a united band of called-out ones *(ecclesia)* — all members one of another. The 'unchurched' Christian is denying in practice what is in principle at the centre of the Christian life. To be an 'independent' Christian is to say you have no need of brethren in the Lord. To join yourself to others in Christ, in contrast, is the admission of need — it is the humility to recognize that you cannot 'go it alone'. You cannot help loving the people that God loves; these are your brothers and your sisters and your mother in the risen Christ (Mark 3:31–34).

It follows, thirdly, that true conversion involves *a readiness to share the joys and sorrows of God's people.* 'Where you go I will go, and where you stay I will stay.' Ruth had a mother (1:8) and probably many other loved ones, but she left them all for what was, humanly speaking, a bleak and unpromising future. For many a young Christian this has been the first great test of faith. The rich young ruler counted that cost and clung to his riches; Moses faced it and 'chose to be ill-treated along with the people of God rather than to enjoy the pleasures of sin for a short time. He regarded disgrace for the sake of Christ as of greater value than the treasures of Egypt, because he was looking ahead to his reward' (Hebrews 11:25,26).

A fourth element in true conversion is *active perseverance in the faith.* Ruth declared, 'Where you die I will die.' In other words, 'My commitment to the Lord, to his people and to their lot in life will lead me to spend my whole life with them.' Death is not seen as the end of that commitment, of course, since it is through death itself that the Christian comes face to face with the Lord. Subsequent events prove Ruth's mettle, but how sad it is to see the falling away of so many who once had a lively interest, it seemed, in the Christian life. It is deeply impressed upon my soul that one of the first influences in my life for the gospel of Christ became an atheist within a month of introducing me to the ministry through which I was later to become a Christian! 'Make your calling and election sure' (2 Peter 1:10). Hold fast the profession of your faith, never wavering 'for it is God who works in you to will and to act according to his good purpose' (Phil. 2:13).

Finally, notice *the vow with which Ruth solemnly sealed her commitment.* 'May the Lord deal with me, be it ever so severely, if anything but death separates you and me.' How easily men and women take vows of membership in the church of Jesus Christ and lightly cast them aside when it suits them! Such a vow is a solemn act of commitment which carries with it the recognition that to break it later will deservedly incur the divine wrath. So it was with Ruth. So it is, in reality, for everyone who professes faith in Christ. To be converted to Christ is to receive him by faith and to realize that to turn away from him again is unthinkable. Hence the nature of the vow: 'May the Lord deal with me . . .'

Let it be asked of you, dear reader: have you 'paid your vows' to the Lord? Do you know what it is to be converted to Christ? Is the God of the Bible your God? Is Christ your Saviour? Do you love the Lord's people? Would you regard, with Moses, 'disgrace for the sake of Christ' as of more value than the treasures of modern materialism? Ruth confronts us with the vital question: 'To whom do you belong?' To the Lord Jesus Christ? Or to yourself or somebody else? Where you spend eternity and the meaning of your life here and now hang upon your answer. 'Believe on the Lord Jesus Christ and you will be saved' (Acts 16:31).

Questions for further study:
1. Why did Elimelech and his family leave Bethlehem? Was this move blessed by God? Compare with Leviticus 26:19,20 in its context.
2. Should Elimelech's sons have married the Moabite girls? Review Deuteronomy 7:3; 23:1–6; Judges 3:6; 1 Kings 11:1; Ezra 9:1; Nehemiah 13:23. What principle applies to Christians in the present day?

3. Why did Orpah turn back and Ruth stay with Naomi? (Ruth 1:6–17. Cf. Romans 2:28,29.)
4. Consider the meaning of Ruth's confession in Ruth 1:16,17.
   a. Why is it improper to apply these words to romantic love? What kind of love is in view? And what kind of relationship?
   b. Distinguish five aspects of conversion to the Lord in Ruth's confession.
5. Meditate quietly upon your own relationship to Christ. Do you have a personal relationship, by saving faith, to him? Speak to your pastor about this if you have any doubts or questions.

References
1. Edersheim, *Bible History: Old Testament*, p. 238.
2. For a complete account of the chronology see L. Wood, *Distressing Days of the Judges*, p. 254.
3. Marriage to a Moabite *outside* of Israel was not *explicitly* forbidden in the law, although Deuteronomy 23:1–6 seems to imply that such marriages would not be permissible (Cf. Deuteronomy 7:3; Judges 3:6; 1 Kings 11:1; Ezra 9:1; Nehemiah 13:23). Wood *(Distressing Days of the Judges*, pp. 256–257) argues that there were permissible marriages. He deals with the relevant passages and points out that the subsequent marriage of Ruth to Boaz proceeded from the assumption that she was a member of an Israelite family, for all that she was a foreigner from Moab.
4. The levirate principle (Deuteronomy 25:5–10) was a provision under which a woman who was widowed, without children from the marriage, was to be married by her dead husband's brother, so that her first son could carry on the name of her dead husband, 'so that his name will not be blotted out from Israel'.
5. Edersheim, *Bible History: Old Testament*, p. 239.

14.
Bethlehem- Ephratah

Please read Ruth 2 –4

'So Boaz took Ruth and she became his wife. And the Lord enabled her to conceive, and she gave birth to a son. The women said to Naomi: "Praise be to the Lord, who this day has not left you without a kinsman-redeemer. May he become famous throughout Israel! He will renew your life and sustain you in your old age. For your daughter-in-law, who loves you, and is better to you than seven sons, has given him birth." Then Naomi took the child, laid him in her lap and cared for him. The women living there said, "Naomi has a son." And they named him Obed. He was the father of Jesse, the father of David' (Ruth 4:13–17).

'But you, Bethlehem Ephrathah, though you are small among the clans of Judah, out of you will come for me one who will be ruler over Israel . . .' (Micah 5:2).

Someone once said that 'If, as regards its contents, the book of Ruth stands on the threshold of the history of David, yet as regards its spirit, it stands, like the Psalms, at the threshold of the gospel.'[1] There are clear intimations of this in Ruth's beautiful confession of commitment to the Lord and to her mother-in-law, Naomi (1:16,17). Rich as it is, this is only preliminary to the real meaning of the life of Ruth as a child of God. Too often the theme of the first chapter has been taken to be the theme of the whole book and the application to the consciences of men and women has been in terms only of a moralistic analogy

118

of total commitment: 'Ruth was totally committed to God and to others in her day, therefore, men and women must be so committed in the present day.' Now, it is certainly true that in Ruth we are pointed, albeit in the shadowy terms of the Old Testament, to what it means to be converted and become a believer. But the whole meaning and goal of becoming a believer is more than merely imitating Ruth the person; it is rather a matter of knowing the one to whom the message of the book of Ruth points. That is to say, we are called to Christ and to the meaning of the gospel for our lives as Christians of the New Testament age, and that means being called to a richer experience of grace and a more explicit knowledge of the Redeemer than Ruth ever had. Christ does not point us to Ruth; rather Ruth points us to Christ. He is the one to whom we are to come in repentance and faith. He is the one in whom we are to live our lives.

This is precisely the point of the last three chapters of Ruth. In them we are pointed to the gospel and we see the wonderful way in which God has worked out his purposes to bring about the advent of the Saviour, and in the same Bethlehem in which Ruth's son was born a millennium earlier. Ruth, you see, is the Mary of the Old Testament and her son is the redeemer of his kin.

Ruth and Boaz

It was harvest time in Bethlehem and since Naomi and Ruth needed to support themselves, Ruth offered to glean in the fields for any grain that might be left after the reapers had harvested the crop.[2] This was allowed for in the law as a provision for the poor and the alien (Leviticus 19:9,10; 23:22; Deuteronomy 24:19). In the providence of God she chose to glean in a field belonging to a relative of her late father-in-law, a man named Boaz. He saw her and when he learned that she had come from Moab with his kinswoman Naomi he spoke to her and invited her to glean in his fields, even to the extent of eating and drinking with the workers and gleaning among the sheaves themselves. This he did because of his regard for her kindness to Naomi. 'May you be richly rewarded by the Lord, the God of Israel, under whose wings you have come to take refuge,' said Boaz to an astonished Ruth (2:1–16).

That day, thanks to her hard work and Boaz's generosity, she gleaned over a bushel of grain and this, when Naomi found out about it, called forth from her spontaneous praise to the Lord for his goodness. She had forgotten what it was to feel the blessing of God; now God awakened her to his continuing loving-kindness. Perhaps also at this time she recalled that Boaz, as a relative, could be the one to redeem them from their difficult circumstances.

The law of Moses made a double provision for the redemption of those of God's people who had become destitute and without heirs. The first provision concerned property and it is found in Leviticus 25:25–28. 'If one of your countrymen becomes poor and sells some of his property, his nearest relative is to come and redeem what his countryman has sold.' This was to ensure that the land of Israel remained in the families to which it had been apportioned upon entrance into the promised land. The second provision insured the continued existence of these families in the first place. Deuteronomy 25:5–10 declared that the brother of a deceased husband was to marry his widow, if she were childless, in order to provide a child, or children, who would continue the dead husband's name in Israel. This is the so-called 'levirate' marriage.

Since there was evidently some property originally belonging to Elimelech which had been sold, and now should be redeemed for Naomi and Ruth, and since because of the death of Mahlon without issue there was an obligation for a kinsman to marry Ruth and raise children who would eventually inherit that property, Naomi now suggested to Ruth that she propose to Boaz that he be her 'kinsman-redeemer' (3:1–9).

Ruth did as Naomi told her. She went at night to the threshing-floor where Boaz slept beside the grain and she laid herself down at his feet. When he awoke in the night she asked him to marry her. 'Spread the corner of your garment over me, since you are a kinsman-redeemer,' was not an invitation to fornication, but a formal proposal of marriage couched in the picturesque language of the time. Ruth was a model of propriety in this and Boaz in his response exhibited also a very affecting gentleness with her. 'The Lord bless you, my daughter,' said Boaz, 'This kindness is greater than that which you showed earlier. You have not run after the younger men, whether rich or poor. And now, my daughter, don't be afraid. I will do for you all you ask' (3:10,11).

Boaz explained to her that he could only accept her proposal if a closer kinsman-redeemer declined to redeem her. He would see to it on the morrow. In the meantime she could remain until morning, but must slip away quietly before dawn. When morning did come, Boaz gave her six measures of barley to take to Naomi (3:11–18).

The next day Boaz went to the city gate (the place where disputes and legal questions were dealt with in the ancient world) and there sought out the nearest kinsman-redeemer to Ruth. There, in the presence of ten witnesses, he suggested to this man that he redeem the land Naomi was going to sell. Thinking only property was involved, the man agreed. Then Boaz dropped the bombshell: if he did so, he would also have the responsibility of marrying Ruth, 'in order to maintain the name of the dead with the property'.[3] This the man declined to do, and thus the way was left open for Boaz. This was sealed by the man removing his sandal and handing it to Boaz — a symbol of his renunciation in favour of Boaz (4:1–8).

Boaz then formally announced his intentions and the elders heard him and blessed them both in one of the most beautiful addresses given to a couple about to be married: 'May the Lord make the woman who is coming into your home like Rachel and Leah, who together built up the house of Israel. May you have standing in Ephratah and be famous in Bethlehem. Through the offspring the Lord gives you by this young woman, may your family be like that of Perez, whom Tamar bore to Judah' (4:11,12).

In other words: 'May you, Ruth of Moab, be a fruitful

mother of Israel.' And so in due course they were married
and a child was born.

> He the childless woman takes
> and a joyful mother makes;
> Keeping house she finds reward.
> Praise Jehovah; praise the Lord
> > (Psalm 113:9, metrical version).

Naomi's blessing

The final section of the book of Ruth (4:13–21) brings
us back to Naomi and shows how the Lord turned the
remnants of her mourning into joy. As Alfred Edersheim
records, 'Naomi now had a "redeemer", not only to support
and nourish her, nor merely to "redeem" the family
property, but to preserve the name of the family in Israel.
And that "redeemer" — a child, and yet not a child of
Boaz; a redeemer-son, and yet not a son of Naomi — was
the father of Jesse. And so the story which began in poverty,
famine and exile leads up to the throne of David.'[4]
Do you remember the Naomi who wanted to be called
'Mara', 'bitter'? 'Then Naomi took the child, laid him in
her lap and cared for him. The women living there said,
"Naomi has a son" (4:16,17). Mara has become Naomi,
'pleasant' once again. We are reminded of the words of
Isaiah the prophet, which our Lord showed were fulfilled
in his person and work:

> The Spirit of the Sovereign Lord is upon me,
> > because the Lord has anointed me
> > to preach good news to the poor.
> He has sent me to bind up the broken-hearted,
> > to proclaim freedom for the captives
> > and release for the prisoners,
> > to proclaim the year of the Lord's favour
> > and the day of vengeance of our God,
> to comfort all who mourn,

and provide for those who grieve in Zion —
to bestow on them a crown of beauty
    instead of ashes,
the oil of gladness
    instead of mourning,
and a garment of praise
    instead of a spirit of despair

(Isaiah 61:1–3).

And the very blessing of Naomi is one which points to Messiah, for the son born to Ruth was one through whom, ultimately, multitudes would be born to God, for Ruth and her son were the lineal ancestors of the Lord Jesus Christ. This is the central meaning of the story of Ruth.

The provision of a Redeemer

The meaning of the book of Judges is crystallized in the book of Ruth and it is, in a phrase, the provision of a Redeemer, who would come in the fulness of the time. 'Even in darkness light dawns for the upright,' says the psalmist. Who was to know at the time that the sins and miseries of Naomi should be swallowed up in a foretaste of Christ? Who was to know at the time that God should give a Redeemer through a foreigner, Ruth? Who would have guessed that out of Bethlehem of the Ephrathites, so small among the clans of Judah, there should arise one who would be the Ruler of Israel? We are pointed to nothing less than the advent of Christ and the salvation which he purchased for his people upon the cross at Calvary. Three things in particular stand out.

First is the great truth that *our times are in the hands of a God of all grace.* God is working out the same purposes which he had in the days of Ruth. These are eternal purposes, purposes of salvation for his people, purposes of glory for his own holy name. This is always a gracious providence for those who love the Lord. Everything that

comes into our lives is going to turn into blessing sooner
or later. This is a tremendous truth for our daily life.
A person to whom the worst affliction is an opportunity
to find the grace of God is unconquerable! Charles Simeon,
the great English preacher of the early nineteenth century,
charges us never to think that our situation is desperate,
or that God has brought us to such a state for evil. 'For, as
the bondage and imprisonment of Joseph were steps to
his highest exaltation, so may our heaviest afflictions be
the appointed means of bringing us to the most exalted
good. "God's ways are in the deep and his footsteps are
not known" and he not infrequently, "makes the depths
of the sea a way for his ransomed to pass over"' (Isaiah
51:10).[5]

Second is the fact that in Ruth we are given a proof of
God's purpose to call the nations to himself. Well might
Ruth sing in the way called for by Isaiah the prophet when
he prophesied of the glory of the church of Jesus Christ:

'Sing, O barren woman, you who never bore a child;
        burst into song, shout for joy, you who were never
                                                  in labour;
because more are the children of the desolate woman
        than of her who has a husband,' says the Lord.
'Enlarge the place of your tent,
        stretch your tent curtains wide, do not hold back;
        lengthen your cords,
        strengthen your stakes.
For you will spread out to the right and to the left;
        your descendants will dispossess nations
        and settle in their desolate cities . . .'
                                            (Isaiah 54:1—8).

The ingrafting of Ruth into the line which gave rise to
Christ symbolizes the comprehensive scope of the gospel.
Ruth is in a sense a mother of the faithful, a witness to the
love of God for people out of every nation in the world.

Third is the fact that *we have a Saviour to whom we
may go.* The kinsman-redeemer of Ruth reminds us of the

eternal Redeemer. Naomi and Ruth faced destitution and ruin and by free grace were redeemed by Boaz. So Christ comes to the lost and blind and weary and offers redemption — a redemption purchased by free grace through death upon a cross. He becomes our kinsman — flesh of our flesh — who 'had to be made like his brothers in every way, in order that he might become a merciful and faithful high priest in service to God, and that he might make atonement for the sins of the people' (Heb. 2:17).

Judges and Ruth, rightly understood, call us to the Saviour, and call us to 'bind our hearts to his service and constrain us to live to his glory'. May God impress this upon our hearts and draw us to Christ by faith. 'For unto us a child is born, to us a son is given, and the government will be on his shoulders. And he will be called Wonderful Counsellor, Mighty God, Everlasting Father, Prince of Peace' (Isaiah 9:6).

Do you love the Lord Jesus Christ? Is he the Prince of Peace in your heart? Do you thirst for peace, for cleansing from sin and for a life that has real meaning and purpose?

'Come, all you who are thirsty, come to the waters; and you who have no money, come, buy and eat! Come, buy wine and milk without money and without cost. Why spend money on what is not bread, and your labour on what does not satisfy? . . . Give ear and come to me; hear me, that your soul may live . . . Seek the Lord while he may be found; call on him while he is near. Let the wicked forsake his way and the evil man his thoughts. Let him turn to the Lord, and he will have mercy on him, and to our God, for he will freely pardon' (Isaiah 55:1–3,6,7).

Questions for further study:
1. What was the purpose of the law of 'gleaning'? (Leviticus 19:9,10; 23:22; Deuteronomy 24:19). What happened to Ruth when she went gleaning?
2. What is the idea of the 'kinsman-redeemer'? Consider the provisions made in regard to property (Leviticus 25:25–28) and the family (Deuteronomy 25:5–10; Ruth 3:1–9).

3. What did Ruth do about this? (Ruth 3:10,11.) Was there anything unseemly about her action? If not, why not?
4. What was Boaz's response? (Ruth 3:11—4:8.)
5. What was the significance of the address of the elders to Ruth and Boaz? (Ruth 4:11,12.)
6. How did this affect Naomi? (Ruth 4:13—21.)
7. Consider the proposition: 'The meaning of the book of Judges is crystallized in the book of Ruth and it is . . . the provision of a Redeemer.'

References
1. Cassel, *Introduction to the Book of Ruth*, quoted by Edersheim, *Bible History: Old Testament*, p. 238.
2. Ruth's statement in 2:2: 'Let me go to the fields and pick up the left-over grain behind *anyone in whose eyes I find favour*,' (italics mine), does not mean that she was looking for a potential husband. It simply means that she was hoping that, in accordance with the law, she would be allowed to glean by the reapers, as indeed she was.
3. The necessity of marrying Ruth, when it was Naomi's property that was in view, was that the property belonged to Ruth in the sense that she, as the widow of the deceased heir, Mahlon, was the one who potentially represented the family of Elimelech and his son. The property could go 'with the hand of Ruth'.
4. Edersheim, *Bible History: Old Testament*, p. 243.
5. C. Simeon, *Expository Outlines on the Whole Bible*, Grand Rapids: Zondervan, 1956, Vol. 3, p. 106.

Other volumes in the Welwyn Commentary Series by Gordon J. Keddie

DAWN OF A KINGDOM
The message of 1 Samuel
Gordon J. Keddie

272 pages ISBN 0 85234 248 9

The absolute sovereignty of God and the triumph of his righteousness are the principal themes of 1 Samuel. In tracing the development of Israel from the anarchy of the period of Judges — from Samuel the prophet and kingmaker through Saul, the people's choice, to David, God's chosen king — the hand of God is seen at work.

ACCORDING TO PROMISE
The message of the book of Numbers
Gordon J. Keddie

224 pages ISBN 0 85234 295 0

The book of Numbers bridges the gap between the exodus from Egypt and the entry into the promised land, when God's people were in transit between past and present, slavery and freedom, as they passed through the Sinai desert. It is about the church in the wilderness, on a journey from promise to fulfilment. As such it has much to teach us on a practical level about trust in God in the face of difficulties, about temptations we face and the faithfulness of God who remains true to his promise in spite of all our waywardness and mistrust of him.

TRIUMPH OF THE KING
The message of 2 Samuel
Gordon J. Keddie

272 pages   ISBN 0 85234 272 1

The history of David gives us a slice of life in the real world. We see people in their true colours: the petty, selfish, murderous, yet fiercely loyal, Joab; the war-lord Abner; the sad, incompetent Ish-Bosheth and the miserable and vicious sons of Rimmon, who murdered Ish-Bosheth in his sleep. And there is David, the man after God's own heart, borne along by his regal calling on the tide of God's providential acts.

Gordon Keddie draws out the lessons of 2 Samuel and encourages us to look expectantly for the blessing of God in our day.